Business Intelligence

Pocket Guide

A Concise Business Intelligence Strategy For
Decision Support and Process Improvement

Colin McGowan

Author   Colin Mcgowan

Title   Business Intelligence Pocket Guide

Copyright © 2011, Colin Mcgowan, Sydney, NSW, Australia

colin@cmbi.com.au

ISBN-13: 978-0987116604 (CMBI Publishing)

ISBN-10: 0987116606

Version 1.0

To my beautiful family, Julie, Ellie, & Genevieve

About

The book

This short book introduces the challenges of creating a successful business intelligence program. I address these challenges from an organisational and business perspective and the content is predominately non-technical. Business intelligence is about the use of technology, but sponsors of business intelligence solutions, who determine the direction and scope of the projects, are generally not technical specialists. Neither do they have to be, because the goals of business intelligence are very much the goals of the business.

When I visit a company for the first time and discuss the potential of business intelligence with managers and executives, the response is invariably one of excitement and acknowledgement of the possibilities. Business managers will say this is the first time they feel an active interest in a 'technology' project. I wanted to capture the common themes of those discussions and present them to a wider audience.

If you are new to business intelligence, this book should give you the confidence to ask the right questions and avoid the common pitfalls of business intelligence projects. If you are a veteran of one or more business intelligence projects, the chances are you have a mixed experience, with some successes but also some disappointments. I hope this book will provide a framework with which to consider past experience and plan future projects with more confidence in the method and outcome.

I favour a pragmatic approach that acknowledges classic methods and best practice, whilst suggesting how to achieve ongoing progress without being a slave to process.

I am particularly interested in the potential for business intelligence in small and midcap companies. Large corporates have always had the resources and specialist skills to support complex and ambitious projects envisaged by much of the existing literature. Today it is possible for just one or two people to make a significant contribution to the business intelligence capability of their organisation, given the right tools and methods.

The content represents my experience of how business intelligence projects work best, formed from observing repeated patterns and behaviours, successes and failures. The material should whet the appetite of a non-technical audience but I hope will also ring true with those who deal with the technical implementation of business intelligence projects.

Who should read this book

This book will appeal to those who want to create a successful business intelligence program and need practical advice expressed in business terms. If you are sponsoring a business intelligence project, you should find I address many of the key decisions you are facing and raise the visibility of others that you may not have considered yet.

Technical specialists who are new to business intelligence will also find the content useful. This book is not an implementation guide but many of the discussions will address challenges that technical and business professionals will tackle together. Seasoned business intelligence consultants looking for a fresh perspective should also find something here. Although some of the content is accepted wisdom in the business intelligence industry, my personal experience over a large number of business intelligence projects has given me cause to question some of the traditional approaches and present another view.

I think the book will be particularly useful for those managing and supporting small and mid-cap companies that do not currently have a mature business intelligence capability. The good news is that business intelligence is within the budget and capabilities of any organisation with the motivation to improve their decision-making and business processes. In fact, smaller organisations may find it easier to gain quick business intelligence successes; this is because the core competencies – knowledge of the business, data, and technology – are more likely to reside in a single person or closely integrated team.

Readers who come from a large company background will also find this book useful. The main difference in large organisations is that some discussions are further complicated by scale; the oft fragmented nature of big companies; and company evolution through mergers and acquisitions. However, the principles and examples here will be equally as applicable at a business unit level in a large corporation, as they are for the organisation as a whole in a midcap corporate.

Contents

ABOUT

The book 3

Who should read this book 4

CONTENTS 7

INTRODUCTION 11

1. INTRODUCTION TO BUSINESS INTELLIGENCE

Business intelligence cocktail 17

Reactive and proactive business intelligence 21

Measuring business intelligence value 29

Business intelligence users 34

Supporting operational systems with business intelligence 39

Summary 42

2. BUSINESS INTELLIGENCE STRATEGY

Introduction to the business intelligence strategy 43

Business intelligence capability 45

Common business intelligence themes 51

Summary 57

3. PROCESS IMPROVEMENT STRATEGY

Introduction to the process improvement strategy 59

Business strategy alignment   60

Identifying a business intelligence opportunity   63

Defining KPIs   67

Prioritising business intelligence opportunities   76

Migration projects   78

Summary   80

4.   DATA STRATEGY

Introduction to the data strategy   83

Data availability   86

Strategies for promoting data availability   93

Data warehouse   103

Extract, transform, and load (ETL)   113

Data ownership   116

Business rules   120

Summary   128

5.   TECHNOLOGY STRATEGY

Introduction to the technology strategy   131

Guiding principles of the technology strategy   132

Business intelligence solution architecture   134

Data storage architecture   137

User interaction   147

Business intelligence tool selection   167

Business intelligence infrastructure   178

Summary   183

6. PROJECT MANAGEMENT

Introduction to business intelligence project management   185

Business intelligence project duration   186

Business intelligence project team   189

Business intelligence project goals   192

Summary   196

FINAL THOUGHTS   199

GLOSSARY   201

RECOMMENDED READING   213

INDEX   215

ABOUT THE AUTHOR   221

Introduction

Business intelligence (BI)[1] and data warehousing (DW)[2] are by no means new disciplines, yet most companies are only just starting to consider their potential, let alone harness it. If you were thinking, 'I'm already way behind the pack because I do not have a corporate data warehouse, and integrated business intelligence suite', you would be wrong!

This is a great time to start planning and implementing a BI strategy. BI software is no longer prohibitively expensive; hardware is getting cheaper all the time; and most importantly, our perception of how data can help us is continually broadening through exposure to the internet.

One trend I find interesting is the growing disparity between our expectations of information and technology for personal use and for work. We use social networking, online retailing, and smart phones in a sophisticated way, assimilating vast quantities of information. We expect instant responses about the best shopping deals, travel directions, news and weather, or the price of shares. However, when it comes to our work, we accept we must wade through a 30-page report, or simply make a decision without the relevant information, because it is not available, or takes too long to source.

Several observations help explain the widespread adoption of technology in our personal lives. Firstly, even

---

[1] Business intelligence (BI, pronounced *Bee-Eye*)
[2] Data warehousing (DW, abbreviation for *data warehouse* or *data warehousing*)

the most technophobic of us will invest time online shopping, social networking, or share trading, because it helps us achieve something we already do, just more effectively. Secondly, the most successful websites and portals make it easy for us to interact with them. They give us just enough information at each step of the process. Finally, they offer services that enhance the experience beyond our traditional expectations, and in doing so, create new opportunities. A good example is the online shopping paradigm of exposing relationships between different products. Customers, who bought the item we are viewing, also bought these other items. This facility is great, both for cross selling and as a research tool. It alters and enhances our traditional experience of browsing a product range.

The qualities we have just identified fit squarely with the goals of BI. BI solutions should support an existing process more effectively by presenting relevant information in an intuitive way. When information is easier to obtain and interpret, we rarely miss the opportunity to exploit it in new ways.

A BI program should start by raising awareness of the possibilities. BI technology uses innovative manipulation and presentation to transform data into something more useful: information. Each incremental improvement in BI technology lowers the cost of entry to companies that had previously found BI software too expensive. It also broadens the spectrum of suitable business problems. There are a number of different components in a typical BI solution and for each one, a range of available tools, most without a budget-busting price tag.

As money is no longer a barrier to entering the BI arena, *what are the challenges? Where do we start the BI journey and what is the end goal?*

Before commoditised BI software became available, companies could still develop bespoke decision support solutions. However, the challenges: development time; data volumes; and data availability, were barriers to all but the largest organisations. Today hardware is significantly cheaper than a decade ago. This means that, theoretically at least, our ability to process data is catching up with our ability to collect it. BI technology has exploited these hardware improvements. Data is also more available as companies improve and extend their internal systems, and through third party web services and open platforms.

With data readily available and BI tools lowering the cost of processing it, many more business processes become viable targets for BI development.

Before we let unbridled optimism takeover completely, it is worth noting that there is a lot of marketing hyperbole about BI tools and outcomes that are neither realistic nor fully representative of the BI lifecycle.

When you attend vendor presentations of BI products, you may hear statements like:

> *"Achieve one version of the truth"*
> *"Consolidate all your data"*
> *"Reverse the proliferation of spreadsheets"*
> *"Remove your reliance on the IT department for reporting and analytics"*

Whilst each one has its appeal to different people in an organisation, these statements immediately oversell the capability of most BI projects and undersell the value of making efficiencies one small step at a time. Each BI project should achieve an array of different goals. Some of them will work towards these vision statements, but we should not scope a BI project or program at this level. Some are side effects of a well-implemented BI strategy, but they should not be the end goal.

BI works best when you take existing and accessible data, then process and present it so that the end user is much closer to a position of informed action than they might otherwise be.

BI and DW projects have a reputation for being risky but they need not be so. The BI strategy outlined in the following chapters is a pragmatic way to build a BI capability within your organisation. The strategy is your reference point, ensuring that every project improves the overall BI capability within the organisation.

First, you must have an informed view of BI as a process. This will help you select the right projects and set realistic objectives. In Chapter 1, we start by looking at the essential ingredients of BI. Having set the scene, Chapter 2 considers the components of a BI strategy and introduces the goal of continuous improvement to BI capability. Chapters 3 through to 5, look at the three pillars of a BI strategy, exploring practical techniques for their implementation. Finally, in Chapter 6 we tie the strategy together through a short discussion of BI project planning. We explore how to align each project to the goals of the BI strategy and how to set goals and measure success of each project.

For the benefit of brevity and clarity, I focus on the most common patterns of BI found in organisations. I started out with the observation that most companies are not even close to exploiting the full potential of a standard BI platform. With this in mind, we focus on what is achievable with this in place.

Innovation within the organisation will yield far greater benefits than constantly searching for the next big thing or technology breakthrough. BI technology is continuously improving but at a far slower rate than our potential to improve business processes with the BI technology currently available. Do not wait for the next product release, latest version, or ground breaking technology that is always just over the horizon. With the concise strategy and practical advice in the following chapters, you can start planning your BI strategy today.

1.   Introduction to business intelligence

BI is the use of specialist technology for decision support and business process improvement. Without the technology, there is no BI. The technology *does* provide the potential to realise huge efficiencies in short timeframes.

That is the short story, and the one that places the technology front and centre. We want to believe it because we know that business processes could be more efficient, and decision making more effective. A technology solution seems both appealing and intuitive. Like any headline, it pays to read the whole story before jumping to conclusions. That story is the focus of this chapter and by the end, you should have a clearer picture of BI and how it works in practice.

Business intelligence cocktail

The *business intelligence cocktail* has a number of essential ingredients. With them in place, a little mixing is all it takes to provide a result that will really impress.

But be warned! This recipe does not respond well to improvisation. Miss an ingredient and risk a bitter after-taste that could bring the BI party to a halt before it has really begun. To avoid a BI embarrassment we start by looking at each ingredient in turn, ensuring that there can be no mistakes when we bring them together for our first BI project.

Business goal/process

The most important ingredient is the business goal. We achieve a business goal via a process and it is the decision points within that process that we wish to support. An old cliché is that BI improves the business process by providing the right information at the right time to the right person. We also need to deliver the information in the right format via the right channel.

Whether it is a sales representative negotiating with a customer; a team leader completing an employee performance review; or a shop manager ordering stock; there is potential to improve the decision process by presenting existing data in a new way.

BI helps us make a more informed decision. The decision is valuable if it furthers some goal or process that is valuable to the business. Identifying candidate goals/processes is the subject of the *Chapter 3 – Process improvement strategy*.

Business subject matter expert

The second ingredient is the subject matter expert. They understand the business process, are responsible for the outcome, and can articulate the high-level goals. Ownership of the process is the strongest motivator for innovation and improvement. The process owner's direct involvement in the BI project is essential to achieving the most effective result.

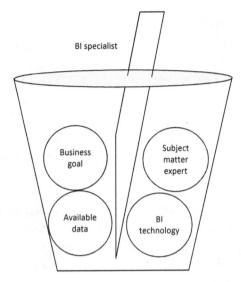

Figure 1 – The business intelligence cocktail

Available data

BI turns data into information to improve the decision making process. The data must be readily available for the BI project to use. Data availability encapsulates more than just the ability to lay your hands on it. The data must be integral, well understood, and in a retrievable format. We address data availability in *Chapter 4 – Data strategy*.

Business intelligence technology

BI technology enables a solution to be realised at a non-prohibitive cost and in a short timeframe. Using specialist software in the right way is what makes successful BI projects so productive. *Chapter 5 – Technology strategy*, provides practical advice on obtaining the right mix of tools to support BI projects.

Business intelligence specialist

The BI specialist is the fifth and final essential ingredient for the cocktail. They play the role of cocktail waiter, tasked with blending the other ingredients together to create the solution. The BI specialist can be a power user sitting within a business function, a technology professional specialising in analytics, or a BI consultant. Crucially, they must have a deep understanding of the specialist technology, design patterns, and best practices to combine the ingredients successfully.

It is the responsibility of the BI specialist to elicit requirements in terms of business goals rather than report or data specifications. The BI specialist should have an empathy and keen interest in the business problem at hand.

I strongly recommend that the BI specialist communicate directly with the subject matter experts and end users to negotiate solutions that play to the strengths of the technology, available data, and requirements of the business. A solution designed with close cooperation between the BI specialist and business process owner will look very different to one where the requirements pass through various intermediaries and cycles of formal documentation. The great potential of BI tools and practices is their ability to solve common business problems in novel ways. It is therefore inappropriate to presuppose a solution design – even at the conceptual level – without reference to the capabilities of the technology. For this reason, the BI specialist should be involved in the requirements elicitation from the initiation of the project.

Mixing it up

The right ingredients are the first essential step. Nevertheless, you would still be disappointed if your cocktail took all night to prepare. The cocktail waiter needs to mix it up at lightning speed. The BI specialist is familiar with the ingredients, can mix without spillage, and has a few nice presentation tricks that will make the cocktail even more appealing to consume. Time to market is crucial in the delivery because it maintains stakeholder engagement. The 80/20 rule is relevant to decision support because improving a decision process is a relative not absolute measure. For a given decision support scenario, some inputs will be straightforward to source and some will be more difficult. Knowing where to draw the boundaries between the solution and the user input is the key to delivering at an acceptable cost.

Reactive and proactive business intelligence

A BI application can improve a business process by monitoring the process and notifying a manager when there is a problem, or by helping the user meet the business goal before problems occur.

A reactive BI application reports the current state of business goals and objectives. The target audience is generally managers who must monitor the extent to which they are meeting objectives. Typical examples of reactive solutions are executive dashboards and scorecards, which show a graphical summary of actual-versus-target KPIs[3] for measures like sales, inventory,

---

[3] KPI (Key performance indicator), see Chapter 3 (section *Defining KPIs*), and *Glossary*

working capital, service levels, and any other metric driven process.

In contrast, proactive BI helps the user meet a business objective. Proactive BI is most effective at the front line of a business. Here lie the tasks that drive the business. If we can perform front line tasks effectively, the high-level business objectives should look after themselves.

A BI strategy can focus too much on reactive reporting. Readers who have seen BI product demos may be disappointed (or perhaps relieved) that I devote little time to executive level dashboards with dials and traffic lights that indicate whether the organisation is about to implode or shoot for the stars. In the ten years that I have worked with users at all levels, I have seen little evidence that a narrow focus on executive dashboards is the best application of the BI budget or technology.

Instead, the incremental improvement in the decision making process at all levels of the organisation results in far more tangible benefits. Each time we build a BI solution for a business process, we can contribute the data we have been working with towards a holistic view to senior management. Using this approach, the executive dashboard becomes an aggregate of the BI strategy progress achieved to date, rather than the end goal. This bottom-up approach to implementation reduces risk because each discrete project delivers value to both operations and management.

Dashboards, scorecards, and reports are often designed with compliance and monitoring in mind. The user – often a manager – will look at a scorecard and may see a red light next to sales. They have the ability to click on the light and see why the sales are down and whose desk they need to start banging! Given managers normally sponsor BI projects, this may not be a surprise, but it misses a big part of the BI opportunity. Before getting too obsessed with KPI monitoring, we should reflect on what percentage of the BI budget we used to help achieve those targets.

Moving from reactive to proactive business intelligence

Consider a Financial Controller (FC) who has a target to reduce banking fees by 50%. She can see that reducing the number of overdraft breaches is the key to reaching this target. The problem is complicated because the bank requires three days' notice to change the authorised overdraft limit. If the overdraft is not required, the company still has to pay additional fees for the facility. Balancing the cost of arrangement fees with the risk of a breach is the decision process that the FC hopes to improve.

A reactive solution might report the current overdraft limit, the account balance, and any known payments and receipts that are still to clear. The FC now has a daily snapshot of how close they are to the overdraft and can take action if she feels they are getting too close.

A proactive BI solution aims to move the decision maker a lot closer to action. The FC is only indirectly concerned with the current overdraft limit, account balance, and difference. What she really wants to know is whether they need to change the overdraft limit and if so, by how much.

Remember we are interested in what might happen in three days from now because of the time it takes to arrange a change. The FC may subconsciously consider a large number of variables when making her decision. We want to formalise these so that the BI application can do more of the legwork.

After an initial requirements analysis, we decide the following information is important.

Table 1 – Data requirements for the overdraft management solution

Data	Rationale	Source system
Average current account balance for the equivalent week, one month ago	We assume that regular events occur in recent history	General Ledger
Average current account balance for the equivalent week, one quarter ago	We assume that regular events occur in recent history	General Ledger
Average current account balance for the equivalent week, this time last year	We assume that regular events occur in recent history	General Ledger
Invoices raised to customers between 30 and 60 days ago	Likelihood of receiving payment from customers	Billing
Planned annual leave for accounts receivable staff in the next week	Likelihood of receipts not being banked or allocated due to staff absence	Human Resources Management
Sick leave currently being taken by accounts receivable staff	Likelihood of receipts not being banked or allocated due to staff absence	Human Resources Management

Data	Rationale	Source system
Number of public holidays in the next week	Likelihood of normal business processes being delayed due to greater proportion of holiday taken by staff and customer staff	Human Resources Management
Supplier orders submitted between 30 and 60 days ago	Likelihood of having to make large unscheduled payments in the near future	Order / Procurement
Planned marketing events for customers in the next 2 days	Customers sometimes bring cheques with them to marketing events as a good will gesture	Customer Relationship Management
Accuracy of predictive value for last week	Reporting how accurate our proactive model has been in predicting overdraft breaches	BI solution historical data

Data	Rationale	Source system
Accuracy of predictive value for last month	Reporting how accurate our proactive model has been in predicting overdraft breaches	BI solution historical data

Having brainstormed all the things that might directly or indirectly affect the chance of going overdrawn, we can then begin to assign weightings and make assumptions about their impact. The final model[4] might state the likelihood of going overdrawn in 3 days and the predicted account balance. Alternatively, we may just display the data in a dashboard layout allowing the FC to assimilate the information quickly and make her own prediction.

We may find we cannot obtain all of the data, in which case at least some part of the decision process will rely on manual effort or assumptions. We may also find that in the early stages the proactive BI is not particularly predictive. Measuring the accuracy of any proactive BI is crucial to determining this. You can use reactive reporting methods to monitor accuracy of previous predictions.

Even with incomplete data, the exercise of using a structured approach to decision making should result in a faster and more consistent process. When we make decisions using a consistent approach, it is easier to measure their effectiveness. Quantifying the effectiveness of existing decisions is an essential step on the path to improving them.

---

[4] Data mining technology is used to build predictive models but a data mining solution is not assumed in this example

BI tools and methods are the ideal candidates for solving this type of data intensive question. The challenges include:

- Data consolidation – from an HR, CRM, Billing, and General Ledger system
- Data processing – complex calculations with large volumes of historical data
- Reporting – reporting the outcome, and providing intuitive navigation of the data

The generic BI solution architecture (see *Chapter 5 – Technology strategy*) has a specialist tool for each of these tasks.

Reactive reporting used proactively

The discussion above may leave you with the impression that reactive BI is of less value than the proactive approach. However, a reactive solution can result in proactive decisions. For instance, a KPI dashboard shows the sales director that sales are below budget, and so he calls a meeting with his sales team to work on a strategy for improvement.

Reactive reporting is generally less complex, cheaper to implement, and is certainly preferable to no BI at all. It is also more transparent and the best starting point in an immature BI project because it is easier to validate the quality of the data. In the early stages of BI and DW projects, data quality is the primary concern for most users.

One final consideration for reactive reporting is the importance of designing metrics with the correct sensitivity. You need to consider how frequently you want to monitor the subject area (see *KPI volatility* example below). The selling point of the dashboard and scorecard approach is that it communicates only the essential information, removing noise. The user need only look at the status of a few gauges and they can monitor the health of the business.

Nevertheless, it is easy to design KPIs that are not sensitive enough to events to provide good indicators of emerging issues or opportunities. By the time an issue emerges on the KPI gauge, it is already known or too late to avoid.

BI in practice

KPI volatility

A CEO uses an executive dashboard to monitor the performance of business units with various KPIs based on financial year-to-date metrics (FYTD). At the start of the financial year, the KPIs are highly volatile and small events have a disproportionate impact on the FYTD metrics. The dashboard is of limited interest to the CEO during these early days.

Towards the end of the financial year, it takes very significant events to move KPIs based on FYTD data. For this reason, the CEO may only refer to the dashboard once a month because nothing appears to change.

Let us assume we could manually compile the dashboard data in a day without using BI tools. It may not be cost effective to automate data integration from across the organisation for a report that is only required ten times a year.

However, we could take that same underlying data and provide the CEO with a far more *finger-on-the-pulse* view of the world. If we want the CEO to look at the dashboard every day, then the dashboard should provide new and interesting insights at the same frequency.

If we show relatively stable KPIs in a gauge or traffic light dashboard, we should supplement the dashboard with the current events that are contributing to those KPIs today. This keeps the dashboard fresh and interesting even if the high-level indicators do not appear to change much from day to day.

Measuring business intelligence value

Setting realistic expectations from the start of the program is the best way to create a sustainable BI capability. However, measuring effectiveness is also a good way to maintain sponsorship for the program. The following sections look at how you might capture the value of some typical BI scenarios.

Quantitative value measures

Report automation

Analysts and power users can spend a significant portion of their time producing regular reports and analysis. Although they are experts in the technology available to them – typically spreadsheets and personal databases – these tools are not ideal for creating and publishing regular analysis.

Because the analysis is complex to compile, the power users often believe there is little scope for efficiencies. Training power users in the BI toolset and assisting in the automation of complex data integration and analysis will produce immediate and quantifiable benefits. Freed from the routine workload, the user can concentrate on analysis or process improvement that delivers fresh insights or value to the business.

Report automation generally creates value over and above the time saved in the preparation. When information is quicker and cheaper to obtain we may find many other opportunities for its use.

BI in practice

Indirect benefits of report automation

I observed firsthand the indirect benefits of report automation during a project to produce a client relationship dashboard. The dashboard displayed a number of KPIs and historical trends and took about 3 hours per client to produce. Only the company's most important clients warranted this expensive analysis.

If the sales or marketing team wanted to see similar statistics for emerging or target clients, they would have to make an ad hoc request. This would be time consuming and showed only a subset of the figures in the dashboard and without the same careful consideration for layout and presentation.

By automating the data integration and layout using BI tools we were able to produce the report for any of the company's clients on demand. This freed up analyst time but also provided an improved service to marketing and sales.

Process automation and support

Process automation is another area where we can make quantifiable efficiencies. Unlike report automation, the users in a process improvement scenario are less likely to be data manipulation specialists. Because of this, significant process efficiencies are often possible with less technical effort than with the report automation scenario.

The difficulty here is spotting the opportunity. Unlike reports distributed by power users, there may be no visible evidence of a manual process. The user is simply doing the work as a way of achieving their primary business objective. Unless you take time to understand their process in detail, you would never know the opportunity exists. In addition, the user is unlikely to admit there is an issue. They may not realise there is scope for improvement or might be embarrassed to admit there is a problem.

The benefits of process automation, as with report automation, are not limited to the time saved by supporting a particular step. A real world example later in the chapter shows how a BI solution to a single accounts receivable process, measurably improved the cash flow for the whole organisation.

Technology consolidation

Never start a BI project with the *sole* aim of making short-term savings through technology consolidation. My experience is that introducing new BI technology eventually reduces reliance on existing equivalent solutions, but this is a gradual process.

Even when the new tools have overwhelming advantages, users comfortable with existing tools will be slow to transition. It is amazing how many dependencies come out of the woodwork if you try pulling the plug, even if you have performed some prior impact analysis. Being too aggressive about promoting new tools may only breed resentment of their use and miss a valuable opportunity.

Moving from one technology to another is an inevitable event in most businesses, and may save money in the long term. However, we should use the transition as an opportunity to review existing requirements, adding value through process improvement. We return to this discussion in the *Migration projects* section of Chapter 3.

Qualitative value measures

If the target process is highly repetitive and operational in nature then quantitative benefits are easier to measure. The benefit of providing BI to less frequent – but nonetheless regular – managerial decisions may initially appear far less tangible. Yet BI normally targets these decisions and the users that make them.

The stepping stone path to improving the decision process

It is easy to claim that BI helps people make better decisions. For all but the simplest business process, improving decision support involves more than delivering a report with graphs and gauges. Figure 2 (below) illustrates the stepping stone path that leads from a semi structured decision process to a structured decision supported by BI.

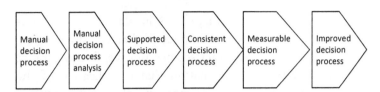

Figure 2 – The stepping stone path to decision support

1. In *a manual decision process*, the inputs vary over time depending on the availability of time or data. We cannot measure the effectiveness of the decision process (as opposed to the decision itself) because the inputs to the decision have not been formalised or recorded

2. During *process analysis*, the decision maker takes a step back from the operational process and considers the ideal inputs for the decision. They may need some guidance from a BI specialist to start thinking about the full range of possible inputs. Chapter 3 looks at this step in more detail

3. In the *supported decision process* phase, we design a solution using the findings from the previous stage. We support the decision by providing consistent data and giving consideration to the presentation. This is our first iteration of BI development for the process

4. Once the decision maker has consistent and reliable inputs for the process they will have time to focus on the possible shortcomings of these inputs. This will lead to further iterations of the BI solution until the decision maker is satisfied with the support. At this point, we have a *consistent decision process*

5. With a consistent process in place, we can focus on measuring the impact of that decision. Again, this is not an exact science but we aim to capture and record information that is indicative of the decision impact. Once in place, we have a *measurable decision process*

6. A consistent and measurable decision process is not necessarily a good one. We just have a better idea of how good or bad it is. This allows us to modify the input variables systematically and assess the impact

This sounds great in theory. However, will it work with real decisions in the real world? It is probably fair to say that most BI projects do not have ambitions beyond the fourth stone – a consistent decision process. I think the benefit of the last two stones in the path comes from applying this thinking to the earlier stages. After all, what is the point in spending a lot of money on decision support if you have not thought about how you are going to measure the real benefit?

Business intelligence users

BI users are not a homogeneous group. This is why you need a variety of BI technologies (see Chapter 5) if you want to support them all. Each BI tool suits a different interaction scenario and is extremely effective if correctly applied. One of the most common mistakes is to push a BI tool beyond its comfort area – akin to using a baseball bat to play tennis, it *might* be possible, but it will *definitely* be frustrating.

Therefore, it is important to identify the user types so that you can deliver the solution using an appropriate method and technology.

Intra company users

It would be wrong to assume there is a one-size-fits-all delivery channel for BI. The table below considers which might be appropriate for different roles within the organisation. As the table indicates, proactive BI becomes more difficult to implement as you ascend the organisation hierarchy. Senior managers and executives often make judgement calls based on experience, informal discussions with colleagues and advisors, and tacit knowledge, all of which is difficult to capture.

Any operational decision point is a target for proactive BI regardless of the role of the decision maker. Operational decisions tend to be more frequent and the categories of information are relatively stable and easy to source.

Table 2 – BI user groups within the organisation

User role	Attributes	BI delivery type	Delivery channel
Senior manager	Time-poor; monitors health of business; reacts using tacit judgement and experience	Reactive	Executive dashboards, static reports
Manager	Monitors operations in detail; relies on information within the business to make decisions	Reactive/ proactive	Operational dashboards, static reports
Analyst	Requires exploratory tools to form and validate hypotheses	Proactive	Data mining model, query tool, spreadsheets
Front line technical, clerical and sales staff	Process oriented. Many decision points per day	Proactive	Business application, operational dashboards

Everyone will use spreadsheets and ad hoc queries from time to time. When used repetitively as part of a predefined process, there is a strong case for a more effective delivery channel. I would imagine that if you took any organisation in the world you would find that thousands of hours a year are consumed performing repetitive data manipulation tasks in spreadsheets. These are ideal candidates for automation and enhancement using other BI tools.

This is not to say that spreadsheets are a bad or wasteful tool. They are perfect for testing a new hypothesis, prototyping reports, or engineering a business process change. The issue comes when the user's time slowly but surely moves from innovation to the repetitive production of that same analysis month-after-month. Analysts and managers are most susceptible to this pattern. They become the victims of their own success and move from being true analysts and decision influencers, to an expensive data manipulation tool. Raising awareness of the capabilities of BI is the best way to bring these processes into the spotlight.

External users

Suppliers and customers are an ideal target group for BI as there is often a mutual benefit to sharing data. Potential opportunities include:

- Cross selling and marketing
- Promoting ease of doing business through increased visibility of process and status
- An added-value service to existing services or products that differentiate you from the competition
- The provision of additional information as a product in its own right

- An incentive for bilateral information sharing

Table 3 describes the three most common types of BI users that are external to the organisation.

Table 3 – Potential BI user groups sitting outside of the organisation

External user type	Attributes	BI delivery type	Delivery channel
Customer of products/ services	Wants to know what other products may be relevant to them and status of their account	Proactive/ Reactive	Data mining (market basket), scheduled reports, dashboards
Supplier of products/ services	Wants to know the pipeline of requirements and reasons for fluctuation in orders	Proactive/ reactive	Dashboards, static reports
Information consumer	Gain immediate value from data you own	Proactive	Data mining model, query tool, spreadsheets

Supporting operational systems with business intelligence

Even though executive dashboards, scorecards, and *slice and dice* [5] tools are at the forefront of any sales pitch for BI, my experience is that BI is at its most powerful when applied to discrete operational processes.

Traditionally, ERP/operational processing systems provide information and reporting for operational processes, but they may struggle to keep up with the continual stream of demands to support new data, reports, and business processes. When this occurs, the choice is an expensive system upgrade or a manual spreadsheet driven process.

BI methods and technology offer a third route that is less expensive and more flexible than modifying core operational systems. Rather than trying to shoehorn additional data into the existing system, a BI approach can capture the data, business rules, and algorithms outside of the system boundaries and then integrate them with the operational data to support the business process.

BI in practice

BI applied to operational processes

A solution I provided a few years back demonstrates the measurable benefits of proactive BI applied to a discrete operational process.

A finance department wanted to improve their cash management. To further that goal, they decided to take a

---

[5] Slice and dice, see *Glossary*

proactive approach to improving the accounts receivable process.

Every day an accounts clerk would receive a number of large cheques from clients. The clerk's task was to apportion each cheque between the many expenses relating to the client's case, professional fees for the law firm, and future costs.

Unfortunately, all the accounts clerk had to work with was a transaction history report parameterised by date and rendered in date order. The manual reconciliations could take hours per cheque, but until it occurred, the firm could not bank the money owed to them.

The new solution requested the cheque value and the case number from the user, performed an extract from the ledger system, and then applied the complex business rules to the transactions to determine the final allocation. The extraction process imported the data to a spreadsheet and displayed the information in a dashboard layout using summary tables and descriptive fields to show the allocation.

Instead of taking hours, the accounts clerk was able to allocate the cheques within 15 minutes by using the new process. The result was a measurable improvement in the cash flow of the firm because they could always bank their fees on the day of receipt.

Business goal:	Improve cash management
Business process:	Allocation of accounts receivable cheques
Decision points:	Determine destination of monies
Subject matter expert:	Accounts clerk

BI technology:	ETL/spreadsheet
Data:	Transactions in billing system

The spreadsheet output was not the end of the process. The accounts assistant still needed to validate the expenses and follow any special instructions that might alter the default allocation. Because we used a spreadsheet to present the dashboard data, the assistant or responsible lawyer could alter the allocation if required, then distribute for approval.

Importantly, the solution brought the accounts clerk much closer to a point of action – banking the cheque.

A reader who comes from a technology background may be tempted to think that such manual processes no longer exist. After all, ERP[6] systems have come on a long way in recent years and people are more aware of the capabilities of technology. My experience is that we continue to create these manual processes every day in every organisation.

However well specified, operational systems will always be one-step behind the business, which must continue to adapt or implement their own unique processes and decision points. BI offers a practical, inexpensive, and more flexible alternative to continual modification of operational systems.

---

[6] ERP (enterprise resource planning), see *Glossary*

Summary

In this chapter we covered the
- ✓ ingredients for successful BI projects
- ✓ differences between reactive and proactive BI
- ✓ methods for measuring the value of a BI project
- ✓ potential user groups of BI solutions
- ✓ use of BI to extend the functionality of operational systems

The key messages from the chapter are:
- ❖ The *business intelligence cocktail* of business goal, subject matter expert, available data, BI technology, and BI specialist, is the best recipe for successful BI projects
- ❖ BI requirements should focus on proactive as well as reactive solutions. We should help users meet their business goals (proactive) as well as measuring their success (reactive)
- ❖ Think about how you will measure the success of the BI project. This will provide a focus and discipline for requirements. Use the stepping stone path to measure the impact of decision support solutions where the benefits are more difficult to quantify
- ❖ BI users are not a homogeneous group. This is one reason why there is such an array of BI end user technologies
- ❖ BI can be a cost effective alternative to extending existing operational systems

2.   Business intelligence strategy

Introduction to the business intelligence strategy

You wake up one morning and decide that your company needs a BI strategy. You are worried about missing the BI party. Alternatively, you may be having a party of your own that appears to be getting out of control!
So, what *is* a BI strategy?

The three pillars of a business intelligence strategy

Three pillars support the BI strategy. For each pillar is a tangible strategy with concrete tasks and objectives. The BI strategy joins the three pillars, which when executed in coordination, steadily increase the BI capability of the organisation.

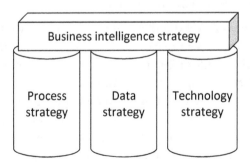

Figure 3 – The three pillars of a business intelligence strategy

Firstly, we must decide how we are going to identify and prioritise opportunities for BI in the organisation. The process improvement strategy in Chapter 3 will provide this direction. Secondly, we need to harness the data assets of the organisation. The data strategy introduced in Chapter 4 addresses the need to raise the availability of data so that it can be utilised for the benefit of everyone. Finally, we must build a technology infrastructure to support the implementation of the process improvement and data availability strategies. Chapter 5 looks at a technology strategy that provides support for this objective.

It is in the early stages of a BI program that we are most vulnerable to making costly decisions, taking the wrong path, or placing too much emphasis on a particular methodology, technology, or vendor. The three pillars guide these early steps providing a reference point for each one of your BI projects. As the momentum and knowledge of BI grows within the organisation, you will form your own procedures and best practices, building on these generic foundations.

What do we cover in this chapter?

Having introduced the three pillars of the BI strategy, the focus for the remainder of the chapter is on subjects that span all three pillars. First, we look at BI capability, not as an abstract concept, but as a practical tool for choosing the right projects at the right time in the BI strategy. The final sections of the chapter identify some common themes and issues that arise in the early stages of most BI programs including sponsorship, empowerment of end users, and the role of the IT department in the BI strategy.

Business intelligence capability

The concept of BI capability is useful because understanding how and why it changes over time should prevent us from picking projects that are too ambitious too early.

In the early stages of implementing a BI strategy we will be:

- discovering a lot of information about key data sources
- performing data extraction work for the first time
- learning how best to apply the BI technology to the business problems

The combination of these factors throws up a plethora of risk, uncertainty, and inefficiency. The three pillars of the BI strategy address the factors that initially limit our capability. Nevertheless, we need to appreciate the following three points from the very beginning.

1. When we start implementing the BI strategy our BI capability will be low and we should avoid long risky projects however compelling the need
2. Our BI capability will improve with BI project experience and at this point we will be able to take on the more complex projects but with a lower risk and more certain outcome
3. If early projects shoot for the stars and fail, sponsors will question the credibility of the entire BI program

Because it is so tempting to jump into the more complex projects, we may need several methods of communicating our BI capability to impatient stakeholders. Yes, we must deliver business value to the user community from the beginning of the strategy, but without taking on unreasonable risk. The following section introduces a BI capability chart I have created to communicate some of these concepts.

The BI capability chart

Figure 4 (below) is a simple way of visualising our ability to develop BI solutions of increasing complexity with the available BI tools and data.

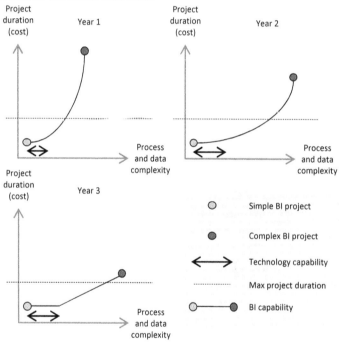

Figure 4 – BI capability charts (Years 1-3)

The three charts describe the changes in our capability to build BI solutions as time passes and we complete our first few BI projects. The following sections consider the components of the charts and the implications for our BI program.

Technology capability

Once we have completed the initial deployment of BI software we should get some quick wins from the capabilities of the technology with little additional effort or risk. The double-headed arrow represents the immediate benefits from the technology. As vendors release new versions of our chosen technology and we acquire other specialist tools, we will make further inroads into business process support; the double-headed arrow expands with the passing of time to capture more business processes as seen in the Year 2 and Year 3 versions of the chart.

It is worth noting that once you have implemented your BI solution architecture (see Chapter 5) you should not rely on further technology innovation to increase your BI capability significantly in the short to medium term. Game-changing technological advances are rare in BI and are generally the result of gradual product evolution, which has suddenly caught the imagination of the market, or been heavily promoted by a major vendor.

BI capability

The technology alone will only take us so far. After that point, our BI capability will determine the projects that are feasible now and those we should delay until our capability increases. The capability curve shows the relationship between the project complexity – encompassing the process and data complexity – and time it will take to execute the project.

In Year 1 (Figure 4, top-left), the capability curve takes a steep and exponential turn upwards after the initial technology gains. This reflects the fact that we have an immature data strategy and will still be learning how to apply the technology to business problems. The practical implication is that many of our ideas for BI projects will be very unpredictable and potentially expensive to execute in the early stages of implementing our BI strategy.

Maximum acceptable project duration

We want to avoid expensive unpredictable projects at the start of the BI program because sponsorship will quickly evaporate if we fail to meet expectations. One practical way to reduce the risk of early disappointments is to set the *maximum acceptable project duration.*

In my experience of BI projects four weeks is a good initial maximum duration[7]. The dotted line in the chart represents this constraint. Put simply, an estimate that greatly exceeds four weeks is likely to be very inaccurate. The steep curve above the dotted line represents the fact that small increases in project complexity can have an exponential impact on cost and duration. We should delay execution of any projects with estimates that exceed the maximum acceptable duration.

Increasing BI capability

If we prioritise projects that sit below the maximum acceptable project duration line, we will subsequently be in a better position to estimate projects of increasing complexity, whilst delivering tangible benefits to the business on these simpler projects. Each short project will increase our knowledge of the available data and BI tools whilst avoiding the risk of expensive project failures.

---

[7] See http://agilemethodology.org for more information on managing project risk

We see the impact of this increased capability in the charts for Year 2 and Year 3. In Year 2, the capability curve is not nearly as steep. This is because we will have identified and analysed a number of data sources, used the technology for real projects, and developed patterns for solving common business problems.

By Year 3, we will have worked with the majority of our data sources and become highly proficient in applying the technology to business problems. New projects will involve incremental improvements to existing solutions and applying proven patterns to new problems. The capability line becomes linear rather than exponential because we have all the information at hand to make informed estimates.

Using the BI capability chart

The chart is an informal tool that represents my experience of some of the dynamics of a BI program. We should not expect to provide exact cost estimates for each candidate project and prove the mathematical relationship between complexity and cost. Instead, we can use the chart to communicate why some business processes are initially better candidates for a BI solution. Equally, we may need to emphasise that other projects, however compelling the need, are simply too risky or expensive to tackle in the early stages of implementing our BI strategy.

Naturally, you will probably find that the most urgent business process improvements are initially above the maximum acceptable project duration. Do not be disheartened by finding your pet project on the wrong side of the line. Try to determine whether some part of the process can be supported using a shorter project that falls within the allowable project duration. Chapter 3 and 4 provide some examples of how we might do this.

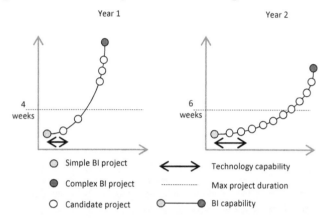

Figure 5 – Plotting candidate projects on the BI capability curve

Figure 5 shows an example of how we might use the chart. At the beginning of the BI program, represented by Year 1(Figure 5, left), we identify five candidate projects. We know that the capabilities of the BI technology are ideal for two of the candidate projects and feel confident that we can deliver them within a couple of weeks. We estimate that the three other projects are probably around six to eight weeks in duration, but acknowledge that BI projects of this duration must have some areas of risk and uncertainty.

By Year 2 (Figure 5, right), several things have changed which alter the content of the chart. Firstly, a lot more candidate projects have appeared. This is because users have had a chance to use the technology and see the results of completed BI projects. The increased visibility of the BI program coupled with our efforts to identify suitable business problems (see Chapter 3) will generate a large number of candidate projects.

Secondly, because the capability curve is not so steep, we can raise the bar on the maximum acceptable project duration. I suggest raising it to around six weeks. It is safe to do this now because we can be more confident in our estimates having gained familiarity with the available data and technology. The shallower curve represents the fact that a slight miscalculation in complexity will not have such an unpredictable impact on project duration as it would in Year 1 projects.

Common business intelligence themes

Sponsorship of the BI strategy

The business is more likely to accept and implement the three pillars if senior managers sponsor and support the process. Sharing data, technology, and process improvement experience across departments and business units is not natural or intuitive in most organisations and yet it can benefit everyone involved. The BI program is a great opportunity to foster this cross function cooperation.

Empowerment of users

A central theme of BI is the empowerment of business users. BI and DW strategies sometimes fall short because of the simple fact that users like to have control over their data. Business units may interpret an IT led BI strategy as an attempt to wrestle control of their data. If users do not feel in control of their data then they will continue to hold their own repositories.

Another facet of user empowerment is the fact that a centralised delivery of BI cannot possibly keep up with user demand for solutions. If we can provide users with the skills and technology to improve their own processes then the BI strategy will realise much greater efficiencies.

Flexible deployment and project initiation

BI requirements change frequently and these changes will only accelerate as the program gathers steam. One successful project will open people's minds to other possibilities. This will result in more requests. A BI strategy must be lightweight and projects agile enough to deliver results quickly. These factors obviously support the argument for user empowerment.

The IT department and business intelligence

Sometimes, I find that IT managers do not have a clear picture of where they sit in the BI technology strategy. Vendors support tools sold straight to the business units and key databases sit outside of their control. Intuitively, they feel that this lack of centralisation and coordination will eventually manifest itself in a maintenance nightmare for their department.

Driving this trend are vendors who exploit the frustration of user communities by claiming their solution requires no support from professional technologists. All too often, the user community just become dependent on the vendor's consultants rather than internal IT resources.

This can be a difficult chicken-and-egg type of problem. The IT department are reluctant to invest money in dedicated BI resources if the business units would prefer to work with vendors. Business units will continue to use external resources if there is no one in the IT department to support them.

Obviously, a complete reliance on vendors misses the opportunity of building the skills and knowledge within the organisation. It means that we must formally scope and cost each new BI project rather than allowing requirements to flourish organically through closer cooperation between departments.

Realistically, even power users may need assistance from time to time, particularly with ETL[8], data modelling and performance tuning. If technology department personnel are available for review and advice then this will enhance the quality and turnaround of BI solutions.

Business intelligence environment administration

It is important to differentiate BI environments from operational systems where it is necessary for the IT department to take a hands-on role in day-to-day maintenance and control, to ensure availability and smooth running of the business.

User communities should have greater freedom to make their own mistakes in a BI environment, especially in the initial stages of a program. The IT department should provide the safety net, for instance by creating backup schedules for key data stores. But we must accept that users may crash the BI server, accidentally delete reports, run ETL processes at inappropriate times, create inefficient cubes, and cause a certain amount of technology chaos as part of a natural learning curve. If we reprimand or patronise these experiments, users will quickly return to spreadsheets and personal databases and BI opportunities will be lost.

---

[8] ETL (extract, transform, load), see *Glossary*

Table 4 – Division of responsibilities between the IT department and the user community for implementing the three pillars of the BI strategy

BI strategy	BI task	IT department	User community
Process	Defining objectives	Advising on data availability and existing solutions	Defining business goals
Data	Increasing data availability	Increase visibility of data across business units. Provide development support for data integration	Own and manage data
Technology	Database and ETL technology	Choose technology. Support configuration and provide training and support. Development work if required by users	Power users can develop solutions. Other users may just specify requirements

BI strategy	BI task	IT department	User community
Technology	User facing BI tools	Create environment and infrastructure. Provide support and examples of best practice if able to	Choose tools. Develop solutions

Project focus

BI is most effective when applied to discrete steps in a business process. Start with a small process or routine decision and support it with a short project with quick results. As your company's competence in the tools and knowledge of the available data improves, you can take on incrementally more complex tasks while still using short iterations. Not every project will meet all its objectives, but any disappointments will be far more acceptable if the project has been restricted to a few weeks development effort and contributes to our capability to execute subsequent projects as part of the wider BI program.

Slave to the strategy

The BI strategy for business process, data, and technology is a point of reference. If formerly you were without a strategy, you are now making decisions within a framework. Whatever approach you use for directing the BI program, the justification for doing it should be that it makes sense within the organisation and has measurable benefits. The strategy is never a justification in its own right.

The best way of avoiding risk and optimising the strategy over time is to start with small projects and quick wins, keeping the majority of the budget and resources in the back pocket for when you are comfortable with the process and outcomes. This raises moral and momentum for the program whilst giving room for manoeuvre if early projects are not as successful as hoped.

Summary

In this chapter, we introduced the:

- ✓ Three pillars for process, data, and technology that, taken together, support the objectives of the BI strategy
- ✓ BI capability chart for visualising our ability to provide cost effective solutions to target business processes
- ✓ Common themes to consider in the early stages of a BI program

The key messages from the chapter are:

- ❖ The three pillars of the BI strategy provide a reference point for making decisions about the BI program
- ❖ BI capability will improve over time. Projects that are initially too complex to solve cost-effectively, will come into range as our knowledge of the data, technology and BI methods improves
- ❖ The IT department should support all three pillars of the BI strategy. However, we should appreciate that BI environments have different characteristics to operational systems and adjust the engagement model accordingly
- ❖ Whichever strategy we use to guide the BI program, we should continue to review its effectiveness and relevance to the business

3.   Process improvement strategy

Introduction to the process improvement strategy

The first ingredient of the *business intelligence cocktail* is the business goal/process that we want to support. The process improvement strategy provides guidance for identifying suitable business problems.

In traditional application development, we start with the problem and then design and build a solution to address it. BI has a slightly different emphasis because we are trying to match the capabilities of the new BI technology with the existing business challenges. We may need to consider a number of candidate business processes before we find a good fit. Once we have matched technology and business process, we must also consider the steps within the process we can efficiently support. With this in mind, the four primary objectives of the process improvement pillar of the BI strategy are:

1. Define a structured approach for identifying process improvement opportunities
2. Define an approach for analysing an opportunity in terms of decision points and data
3. Create a framework for prioritising opportunities
4. Foster a culture where people question their own processes (as opposed to other peoples) and are rewarded for innovation

What do we cover in this chapter?

We start the chapter by describing a straightforward way to align business processes with the objectives of the organisation. This provides a useful reference point for proactive and reactive BI solutions.

We then look at a couple of practical techniques for deriving BI opportunities from the wider objectives and challenges of an individual user or user group. The requirements elicitation and decision point analysis described in these sections will be most useful for proactive BI solutions.

Reactive BI solutions usually involve measuring progress against predefined objectives. The section on defining KPIs provides guidance for creating useful and maintainable targets and metrics.

Having considered ways to identify requirements and opportunities for BI solutions, we then look at criteria for prioritising them. We round off the chapter with a short discussion of why software migration projects that use BI technology, may not realise the full benefits we would normally expect of BI projects.

Business strategy alignment

BI works best when we align the project goals to the objectives of the organisation. Most successful companies will have a formalised business strategy in place. Managers at various levels will seek to implement it. A good starting point for a BI strategy is to take an organisation chart and augment it with these strategic objectives and supporting operational processes.

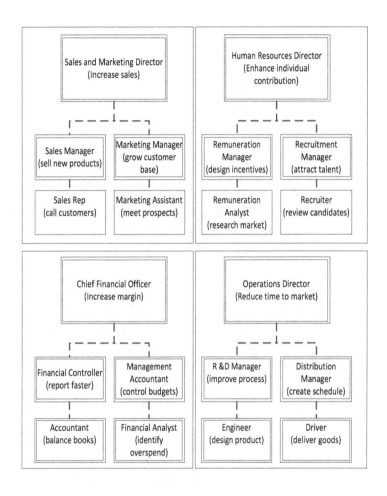

Figure 6 – Aligning the BI strategy to business goals

It is helpful to see the whole organisation on a single chart. Strategic goals in different departments are often interrelated. Where interrelationships exist this is fertile ground for BI because it creates an incentive to share data and information across business units and departments.

We can use the organisation chart for reactive or proactive BI applications. For a reactive solution, we can map the hierarchy of business objectives and processes to a hierarchy of KPIs and metrics. The relationships between the different levels of the hierarchy will translate well into inactive reports or dashboards that give the user the ability to navigate from a high-level target to the underlying operational data and process level metrics. For proactive BI solutions, the organisation chart provides a list of candidate business processes with the additional assurance that the processes do actually support the primary objectives of the business.

BI in practice

Alignment of business objectives across departments

The director of operations has a goal to reduce a product's time-to-market. The sales and marketing director's goal is to increase sales. This is an example of where strategic goals are in alignment.

If operations can build and deliver products more quickly and predictably, sales representatives can create new opportunities and manage customer expectations.

Publishing product development data and progress to the sales team may optimise the planning of marketing and pre-sales activity.

Identifying a business intelligence opportunity

Having documented the business goals on the organisation chart, we can start to hone in on BI opportunities. Good BI solutions require those involved to think imaginatively about how they can improve the way they work. A brainstorming session involving people from different levels of the organisation is a very effective way to assess the feasibility of a project. Senior managers can provide the vision statement, access to resources, and clarity about objectives. Those in operational roles can provide guidance on the availability of data, nuances of business processes, and perceived roadblocks to change.

Business intelligence requirements elicitation

When I interview a manager or subject matter expert about requirements for a new BI project, I like to start by discussing the domain in broad terms. Often, the conversation will begin with the expression of an intractable problem that a dozen people have tried – and failed – to resolve. The stakeholder expresses the perceived solution to the problem in detailed terms, and with great optimism that finally – thanks to the miracle of BI – they will get a successful outcome. Alternatively, the stakeholder uses the problem as a challenge to BI as a product or methodology: 'we have tried to solve this a dozen times, now let's see if BI can do any better'.

It would take a bold ego or a bad case of hope over experience to think that there is an easy fix to something that has collectively baffled an organisation for a number of years. The best policy is to acknowledge the difficult nature of that problem and steer the conversation towards a high-level discussion of the business unit or department objectives.

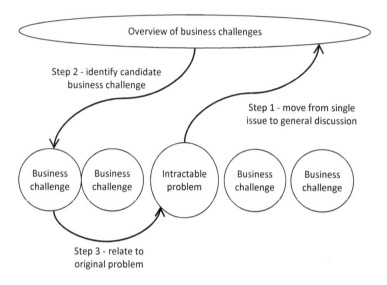

Figure 7 – Identifying opportunities for BI through an overview of business challenges

It is very likely that elements of the original problem will emerge during this more general discussion, but expressed in different terms and with far less emphasis on a solution (which you have already acknowledged is impractical). A BI opportunity is always easier to spot when we have sight of the full landscape for the business domain. When the opportunity comes into view, then it is time to have a more detailed discussion about potential solutions and the contribution they could make to the business. What is interesting is that you often get around to partially resolving the original problem. Typically, all problems encountered during a business process are in some way interlinked.

Removing defensive barriers to change

We all like to think we are doing the best job we can in the circumstances. Business process analysis requires us to step back from the natural instinct to say that our process can only improve if dependencies improve. Instead, we must focus solely on our own objectives.

A top down approach to process improvement analysis can help in these circumstances. If senior managers admit that they could do a better job, and how, then the barriers can start to come down at all levels throughout the organisation. If on the other hand, they start from the premise that others must improve first, BI adoption will be more difficult to sell throughout the organisation.

Decision point analysis

Once we have a candidate business process, we must identify decision points within that process. We may need to apply further decomposition to those decision points. Eventually, no matter how amorphous the original decision, we will get to a point where the decision will rely on some tangible data.

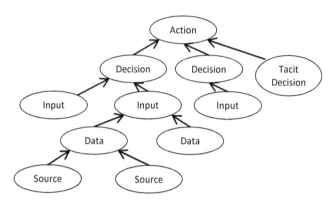

Figure 8 – Mapping data to decisions

Having brainstormed the decision points, sub-decisions, and information requirements, we can now start to hone in on the relevant data. This is where we have to apply pragmatism to the solution requirements. Automating data acquisition is the most expensive part of a BI project. In the early days of your BI strategy, when you do not have the benefit of data integration from previous projects, the cost of data acquisition will be relatively higher.

For each piece of information required by the business process, we must determine the source and then approximate the effort of retrieving it. Source system experts and power users are normally the best people to guide our thinking here. With this analysis complete, we can determine which parts of the business process we can support.

Defining KPIs

A KPI encapsulates a metric and a target. A call centre might have a target to answer 90% of calls within three minutes. In this case, the metric is *percentage of calls answered in less than three minutes* and the target is *ninety per cent*. The KPI reports the variance between the actual value of the metric and the target; this provides a quick way to monitor the health of the business process.

The discipline of creating KPIs is useful in itself. It entails defining relationships between business goals, business processes, and data – vital ingredients of the *business intelligence cocktail*. Figure 9 shows the relationships between the various inputs that we should consider when defining KPIs.

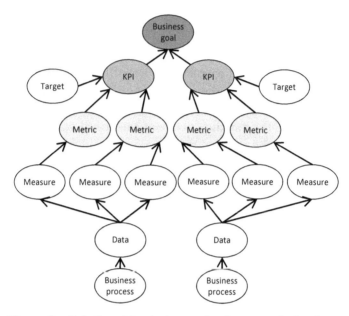

Figure 9 – Relationships between business goals, business process, and data

The business goal is the starting point for defining KPIs. It provides the focus to ensure we are measuring something of value to the organisation. Continuing with the call centre example, the business goal might be to raise customer satisfaction. Having stated the business goal, we can then look at business processes that support the goal. A KPI measures a business process, but the target will be set with reference to the business goal, which is why we need to identify this first. The final step maps the data requirements of the KPI to the data produced by the business process. In the call centre example the *data* is the log of calls, the *measure* is the wait time for each call, and the *metric* is a calculation of the percentage of calls answered within 3 minutes. In this example, the business process provides all the data we need to monitor the KPI, but we cannot assume this will always be the case.

We now look at each of the steps again relating them to the organisation chart introduced earlier in the chapter.

Quantify the objective

As we stated earlier, the business goals are the starting point for creating a set of KPIs. I have reproduced a section from the organisation chart below showing the business goals (strategic and operational) for the sales and marketing function.

Figure 10 – Sales and marketing organisation chart and business goals

The first and most obvious step is to quantify the objectives in the chart. The table below provides this information.

Table 5 – Creating measurable targets for business goals

Goal description	Goal target
Increase Sales	Increase sales revenue by $1 million from previous year
Sell new products	$500K for new product sales
Grow customer base	$750K for new customers; $250K growth for existing customers
Call customers	Call 500 existing customers about new products
Meet prospects	Identify and meet with 100 new target companies

We want to see traceability of strategic objectives through to operational processes in the organisation. The strategic objective is for a $1 million increase in revenue over the previous year. We expect half to come from sales of new products and half to come from growth in sales of existing products. Seventy-five per cent of the revenue growth across new and existing products will come from new customers, with the other twenty-five per cent coming from growth in existing customers.

Identify data

We need to ensure we are tracking the data necessary to measure the KPIs. The table below maps the goals to the data requirements.

Table 6 – Mapping KPIs to available data

Goal description	Goal target	Required data
Increase Sales	Increase sales revenue by $1 million from previous year	Sales this year; sales previous year
Sell new products	Increase new product sales by $500K	Product release date; sales by product
Grow customer base	Sell $750K to new customers; Increase sales to existing customers by $250K	Customer start date; sales by customer
Call customers	Call 500 existing customers about new products	Log of calls recording product and existing customer
Meet prospects	Identify and meet with 100 new target companies	Log of meetings with company name

In the current scenario, we will have no problem calculating sales for the current and previous year using existing operational data. However, we may not be capturing phone calls, customer start dates, and meetings, in a structured way. If the business process does not capture the data we need to measure it then we have a missing link in the relationships shown in Figure 9. This will make it difficult to monitor the KPI for the process and we should address the issue as part of the data strategy.

Defining metrics

Having agreed a target and identified the data, we can define the metric used to track the KPI. Generally, you need to include an element of time so that you can track the progress against the KPI throughout the relevant period.

Sale Target Variance % = ((Sales YTD – Sales Previous YTD) - (1,000,000 / 365 * Days elapsed YTD)) / (1,000,000 / 365 * Days elapsed YTD)

Visualising KPIs

A KPI is often visualised as a traffic light. We define the behaviour of the traffic light display by creating bands as in the following example:

IF Sale Target Variance % >= 0% THEN Green

IF Sale Target Variance % >= -15% THEN Orange

IF Sale Target Variance % < -15% THEN Red

Another alternative is to show the KPI using a gauge with an arrow or line marking the current value of the metric and the bands defined as regions on the display.

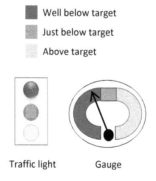

■ Well below target

■ Just below target

■ Above target

Traffic light   Gauge

Figure 11 – Two visualisations of a KPI well below target

Static, dynamic and comparative KPIs

KPIs can be powerful when used in moderation but the process does have shortcomings. Firstly, it is time consuming to agree targets and maintain them. Secondly, if market conditions change we may have to review all the targets once again. Finally, we often lose sight of the original business logic used to create the target. When a KPI is below target, we must first check our rationale for setting the target before deciding what to do about the variance. One solution to these issues is to use a combination of static, dynamic, and comparative KPI targets in the organisation. The following sections define each of these KPI types and explain when it might be appropriate to use them.

Static KPIs

A static KPI has a fixed target that we will not change for the life of the KPI. For instance, a company decides that the revenue target for next year is $100m. The company uses the revenue target to budget costs and strategic projects and so a lot depends on meeting the target. Static KPIs are appropriate for high-level targets because there are not too many to maintain, and we would not adjust them without very careful consideration.

Dynamic KPIs

A dynamic KPI uses a formula to calculate the target at the time we report it. This means that the KPI target can change if the inputs for the formula change. Following on from the previous example, the company may spread the revenue target of $100m across the one hundred retail outlets based on the overall percentage of the revenue contribution for the previous year. Therefore, a retail outlet that generated one per cent of revenue for the company in the previous year would have a target of $1m this year. If there is a change to the $100m target, the retail outlet targets should automatically update.

We should implement dynamic KPIs whenever we have to create a large number of targets based on similar inputs. In our example, the formula may not be appropriate for some retail outlets, but this should not prevent us applying it to the majority. We can always create exception reports whilst benefiting from a more dynamic model. The greater the number of potential targets, the more compelling the need to avoid manual target definitions.

Comparative KPIs

A comparative KPI derives a target by looking at the current performance of comparable entities. Comparative KPIs are very powerful for analysing the performance of highly granular components of the business like individual customers, employees, or products.

Our example company has defined a number of static KPI targets to monitor how quickly their suppliers deliver orders. The problem is that all the suppliers are way behind their targets because they all depend on a group of factories that are having capacity issues. Reporting against the static KPIs becomes meaningless at a supplier level. What the company really wants to know is which suppliers are relatively more efficient given the pervading market conditions. Instead of using static targets, the company defines a comparative KPI target based on the median delivery days of similar supplier orders.

BI in practice

Defining dynamic KPIs

An advertising agency wants to set targets for all its clients. The agency has over one thousand active clients across a range of industry sectors.

The agency does not have time to define a target for each of the clients but does want to track the performance of all clients and report exceptions. They decide the following criteria are important for setting the targets:

```
Sales for the previous year
Inflation rate
Economic growth rate
Industry growth rate
```

They define the sales target for the clients as:

```
Sales target = sales previous year *
  (1 + inflation rate +
  economic growth rate +
  ((industry growth rate -
  economic growth rate) / 2))
```

The company records the industry type for each of the clients and uses this to determine an adjustment based on 50% of the difference between the industry growth and standard growth figure. They periodically download the latest growth rates and inflation data from a government website and incorporate the data into the KPI calculation.

Later they decide that they want to adjust the target dynamically based on their own sales growth data. The new target incorporates an adjustment that calculates the average sales growth for the clients in the same industry sector over the last 6 months. This benchmarks each client against the average sales performance of the other clients in the same industry.

We often consider all these factors when defining KPIs but the KPI becomes truly dynamic when we include this business logic in the BI solution so that we do not have to maintain targets manually.

As well as reducing maintenance, the method increases transparency of the targets. Exposing the business logic, makes it easier for people not involved in setting the targets to interpret the results.

Prioritising business intelligence opportunities

We should prioritise low risk, short projects, that increase our BI capability. A project is more appealing if it helps us drive the objectives for each of the three pillars of the BI strategy. The following sections align to the chapters of this book, each one influencing our capability to acquire and mix the ingredients of the *business intelligence cocktail*.

Process improvement – stakeholder availability and engagement

Some users are early adopters of new practices whilst others are more sceptical of change, preferring to see concrete benefits before altering their working practices. A stakeholder who is predisposed to risks and new opportunities is more likely to ride out the inevitable teething problems of a new solution, without undermining confidence by advertising issues to the rest of the organisation.

Data – available data

If the data is difficult or time-consuming to obtain, then better to leave the challenge until the team has undergone a few BI solution iterations. There are enough challenges in seemingly straightforward solutions without adding known ones into the mix. Data should become increasingly available as the organisation's data strategy gathers momentum. Until that time, it is best to pick the low hanging fruit.

Technology – BI technology familiarity

Projects that play to the technical strengths of team members are clearly less risky. If the BI specialist has greater experience in ETL than dashboard design, then a project aimed at analyst users – where you can deploy an ad hoc analysis tool with minimal front-end design – is more likely to succeed than one for senior managers.

Project duration

3 – 4 weeks is the maximum duration I would advise for each project in an immature BI program. At the end of the project, there should be tangible benefits to users. We should de-scope or delay a project with a longer anticipated duration, until we have had a chance to assess the outcome of shorter projects.

Migration projects

A common mistake is to call a migration project a BI project, just because it uses BI technology. Typically, there will be a collection of reports and processes created in a legacy or tactical environment. The mission statement is to convert and transfer these reports onto the new technology. We use the existing reports as a specification for future requirements. The rationale is that they are unambiguous and we can give them straight to the development team, without the need for too much stakeholder engagement.

This approach misses the point of BI technology, which is to solve the business problem in a novel and efficient way, using the tools to their best capability. Report specifications do not communicate the end goal, nor do they specify how the user will engage with them. Moreover, it is my experience that the majority of reports over 6 months old have lost much of their initial value; this is because the data has become tacit knowledge, or simply not relevant. People move on, but we continue to produce the reports because we always have. Suddenly the reports are indispensible in their current form because Bob must produce the report for Sue, who needs to get the report to Dave, who must send it on to Jane. Jane's secretary then takes it from her in-tray and deposits it in a filing cabinet, or worse still, a waste-paper basket!

To conclude, report specifications alone do not represent a good input for a BI project because *we do not know if*:

- the reports are used (there may be several layers between the initial report recipient and the decision maker)

- the reports are an end goal or simply a stepping stone to further analysis and data discovery
- the reports represent the best way of supporting the business process with the new BI technology

Recall the *business intelligence cocktail*. The missing ingredients in many migration projects are the involvement of the subject matter expert and the explicit identification of a business goal.

Summary

In this chapter, we looked at the process improvement strategy in more detail. We covered:

- ✓ Alignment of BI requirements to the organisation's business goals
- ✓ Methods to identify and analyse a business process as a candidate for BI support
- ✓ Defining static and dynamic KPIs
- ✓ Factors that should influence BI project priority
- ✓ The differences between a technology migration project and a BI project

The key messages from the chapter are:

- ❖ Documenting business goals using an organisation chart raises the visibility of shared objectives that cross business units. This in turn promotes data sharing, a key objective of the data strategy
- ❖ Each business process or decision is comprised of a number of elements. A BI solution may support one or more of these elements within the process, but we should consider each one separately in relation to the available data and return on investment
- ❖ KPIs measure a business process in relation to a business goal. We can only monitor the KPI if the business process captures the data required to measure it
- ❖ Dynamic KPIs are more robust in the face of changing business conditions because they use a relative benchmark

❖ Short projects with highly motivated users and available data are the best candidates for early iterations. The project should also play to the technology strengths of the team to build confidence and moral

❖ Migration projects are an opportunity to review business requirements, and step back from legacy deliverables. Simply converting a set of reports to another technology is a missed opportunity to exploit the capabilities of a new tool set

4.   Data strategy

Introduction to the data strategy

BI solutions process and present existing data to provide fresh insights, reducing the time and resources required to reach a point of action. However, acquiring data can be difficult and expensive. In fact, when we first start implementing a new BI strategy, the cost of data acquisition may be a barrier to many of our candidate projects. For this reason, the data strategy is an essential pillar of the overarching BI strategy.

Throughout this book, I use the term *data availability*. This umbrella term covers the factors that determine the effort and cost of using the data. If data availability is high, it should be relatively inexpensive to use the data in our BI solutions. Conversely, if data availability is low then acquiring the data for the BI solution will be expensive and risky. The data pillar of the BI strategy has one simple aim:

Increase the availability of data to everyone in the organisation

A data strategy does not have a discrete beginning and end. Like the process improvement strategy, it is a continuous commitment. The goal is to improve the availability of useful data, thus lowering the bar to subsequent projects that also require it.

What do we cover in this chapter?

We start the chapter by discussing common factors that reduce data availability in every organisation. We then consider practical strategies to increase data availability by tackling each one of the availability factors in turn. DW is currently the most widely accepted method of increasing data availability and so we discuss the characteristics of a DW that make it an ideal data source for BI solutions. The final sections of the chapter discuss some of the challenges of implementing a data strategy including ETL, data ownership, and defining business rules.

Although the title of this chapter may sound technical, I keep the discussions practical and business oriented. The data strategy is predominantly about raising awareness of the value of data as a business asset. We need to appreciate the business issues before we move to technical solutions.

Data strategy or data warehouse strategy

Some readers may question the title of this chapter. Is a data strategy just a DW strategy by a different name? A DW will be a central aspect of a data strategy in most organisations but the two concepts are not identical. The data strategy starts from the premise that a BI solution may use any data stored inside or outside of the organisation. It is a secondary question as to whether we need to put that data in a DW as an intermediate step to making it available to BI tools. The goal of the data strategy is to increase the availability of the data irrespective of the location. To illustrate this point, we consider some examples of where the BI solution may extract the data directly from source.

Data outside of the DW

The following scenarios are just some examples of where we may choose not to use a DW in a BI solution. A DW in a large corporate environment may be difficult and expensive to change but we should not automatically discard BI projects just because the DW does not currently hold our target data.

Analytical databases

The increasing power and capacity of end user tools and analytical databases make it practical to consume large volumes of data outside of a formal DW environment. For tactical projects, proof of concept, or speculative analysis, it is often viable to move the data straight from source into the BI tool.

External data

The variety and volume of data that is available outside of the organisation is another reason to consider data outside of the DW. It may be expensive, impractical, or unnecessary to duplicate all these potential sources in the corporate DW. BI tools can combine data from the DW and external sources without the overhead of a formal DW project.

DW update schedule

We may need to go straight to the source system if the BI solution needs to use the latest operational data and this is not available in the DW. Changing update schedules in the DW itself may not be straightforward and the cost may be prohibitive for a short BI project.

Data availability

Data availability encapsulates all the factors affecting our ability to use the data for a BI solution. In this section, we explore some of the most common factors that affect availability.

Visibility

Visibility within the organisation

If you do not know the data exists, you will not specify a solution to use it. This is a very common situation in most organisations. Often people in different departments or business units have absolutely no idea what is stored in the operational systems used by other areas of the business. Because this does not appear to affect their operational processes, there is little motivation to learn.

Just as common are personal data repositories, often invisible even within a business unit or team. They manifest themselves as spreadsheets or personal databases and may have a critical role in supporting the owner's business process. The owner may be reluctant to share these sources because they do not want to support a service level agreement where others expect them to update it to their schedule. Equally, they may never have considered that the data might be valuable to others.

Visibility of the outside world

Invisibility of data within an organisation has always been commonplace, but we may also be unaware of the increasing variety of useful data that sits outside of the organisation.

Web services and data provisioning services provided by government and private companies, are a very efficient way of improving the availability of reference and statistical data. Many of the government services are free. The cost of buying lists of addresses, companies, stock exchange, and weather data, to name but a few, is far lower than the cost of trying to cleanse poorly maintained reference data during ETL development.

Industry survey results are an example of data that is generally visible to at least some people in the organisation, because they contribute the company's data to the survey provider. However, there can be a missed opportunity to capture the results in a structured format and share them with the rest of the organisation.

Data quality

Data integrity

Data integrity is the extent to which the data conforms to a set of formal constraints and business rules. A 3NF[9] database design is the most common way of enforcing data integrity. The sample customer table below demonstrates common problems found in data without constraints.

Table 7 – A table of customers with data integrity issues

Name	Age	Gender	Occupation
Amy Dracula Adams	25	Female	Teacher
Jimmy Vampire Jones		male	
Henry Wolf man Hope	Builder	MALE	20
Amy Dracula Adams	Twenty Five	F	Teacher
	5	M	Lawyer

---

[9] 3NF (third normal form), see *Glossary*

Integrity problems include:

- Duplicate rows in the table. Is it likely that we have two twenty-five year old teachers called *Amy Dracula Adams*?
- Missing data in the *Name, Age,* and *Occupation* columns for some rows
- Incorrect and inconsistent data in the *Age* column. If we wanted to find the average age of our customers, the jumbled mix of numeric and character data would hamper our analysis
- Data allocated to the incorrect column.
- Inconsistent representations in the *Gender* column of the two valid values
- A poor choice of data types for representing the *Age* of customers

This type of table is an ETL developer's worst nightmare! The problem only gets worse when you introduce more tables and try to relate customer data to other areas like sales or address lists.

A well-designed and maintained operational database would avoid all these problems. In reality, not all useful data is stored in an operational database. Even when it is, we may still turn to unstructured sources if they are a more current or frequently updated record than the operational system. There is often a strong motivation to use semi-structured repositories, but it is almost inevitable that a manually maintained spreadsheet of more than a few hundred lines will have at least some of the issues seen in the table above.

Data accuracy

Constraints can only go so far in preserving data quality. The following table is an improvement on our original example but still has issues.

Table 8 – A table of customers with data accuracy issues

Name	Date of birth	Gender	Occupation
Amy Dracula Adams	15-Jan-80	Female	Teacher
Jimmy Vampire Jones	25-May-65	Male	Actor
Henry Wolf man Hope	27-Aug-73	Male	Builder
June Dread James	02-Mar-82	Female	Teacher
Terry Troll Timms	25-May-65	Female	Lawyer

The data has consistency, but accuracy is still an issue. In the real world:

- Amy Dracula Adams has quit teaching to work as a security guard on the graveyard shift
- Terry Troll Timms is a man not a woman
- Jimmy Vampire Jones was born on 30-Dec-1958 but somehow Terry's birthdate has been entered instead

These data correctness issues are more difficult to spot but will obviously affect the quality of our analysis and reporting. When users do not trust the data, they will not use it. The data continues to be effectively unavailable even though it is accessible.

Security

Security is frequently a barrier to data availability. You know the data exists but it is not accessible. Statutory obligations, personal privacy, industry standards, or protection of intellectual property may all be legitimate reasons for this.

However, organisations will interpret these standards differently and in ways that will affect the ability to share data. From my observations, it appears that security and access to data within an organisation – we are not talking about exposing the information to the world at large – is a cultural part of the organisation rather than specific to a particular industry or set of standards. Put simply, some organisations have a culture of trust, expecting their employees to act responsibly with the data, and some prefer to avoid the risk by exposing only that which is essential for each person's immediate responsibility.

The most effective BI solutions utilise data from across business processes to provide a broader perspective on the decision. As with our Financial Controller example in Chapter 1, where we considered HR, CRM, and GL data, many decisions would benefit from having more exposure to processes in other business functions.

Data source structure

Common data source structures include relational databases, XML documents, binary word processing documents, proprietary spreadsheet structures, text files, and media files for music and photographs. Sometimes the document type can come in a number of data structures. For instance, a word processing document can be stored as an XML document or a binary file format.

It is possible to make some reasonable assumptions about other availability factors once you know the data source structure. The following table provides some relative indicators for common data sources.

Table 9 – Availability factors for common data source structures

Data source type	Structure	Interface	Tools support	Visibility	Integrity
Relational database	3NF tables and columns	SQL	Very high	High	High
Multidimensional database	Dimensional model	SQL, MDX	High	Med	Med-High
XML document	XML	XML	High	Low	Low-High
Text file	CSV, fixed width	File	Med	Low	Low-Med
Word processing document	Binary, XML, HTML	API, XML	Low	Low	Low
Spread sheet	Binary, XML	API, XML	Med	Low	Low-Med
Web page	HTML, XML	HTML, XML	Med	Med	Low-Med

Non-existing data

Non-existing data for our purposes is data or information that was once known and possibly recorded, but is now lost with the passing of time. We may not record the data, as with the thought processes of a manager making a decision; or we may record, but subsequently overwrite it, as with a database field that records the current state of an entity.

The purpose of identifying non-existing data is firstly, to draw a line at where BI can support a business process at the current time; and secondly, to lay the groundwork for improving data availability by capturing the data for future use. In the early stages of a BI program, we may find a number of our ideas require data that does not exist. These ideas should feed into the data strategy where we determine appropriate methods for capturing the data going forwards. The following example is a common scenario of non-existing data.

BI in practice

Analysing our analysis – data that is never captured

Recently, I was discussing industry survey data with a marketing analyst. The survey provided detailed statistics about sales of the company's products and their competitors' products at a national and regional level. The marketing department used the data to see how they were tracking within their industry.

The analyst explained to me that they discussed the results in a meeting and could normally correlate unusual trends to a specific promotion, television advertising campaign, or new product release.

I was curious to know whether they recorded these insights in a structured format for retrospective analysis. I was not surprised to find that they did not. We review reports, draw conclusions, and then move on. We might take meeting minutes, but we rarely analyse the effectiveness of our analysis!

The conclusions we draw from analysis are often the most valuable data for looking at trends. We could use a history of these inferences to quantify the value of advertising or predict the impact of future industry events.

Update timing

Update timing can be crucial to data availability. For instance, it is very easy to get free share price data from the internet as long as you can accept a 15-minute delay. For people who want a rough indication of their portfolio value, this delay is acceptable. For a professional trader in need of real time information, the delay means the data has little value.

A similar scenario is common for operational systems. Good quality data may exist in the system, and be easy to retrieve. However, if the record keeping process occurs a week after it was completed in the real world, this is too late if we need to know what happened yesterday.

Strategies for promoting data availability

In the previous section, we looked at factors that influence the availability of data. We now consider those factors once again, this time looking at methods to raise availability.

Visibility

Increasing the visibility of data should be the first task in the data strategy. It has the distinct advantage of being a relatively quick and inexpensive process. Practically speaking, we can start by creating a master list of data repositories and publishing it to the company. We can request a short interview with data owners or ask everyone to complete a survey. The process should be a quick painless exercise so that colleagues do not see it as a burden or an intrusion of privacy. At this stage, we do not need a blow-by-blow account of every column in every database and spreadsheet.

You may end up with something similar to the table below. We aim to keep detail to a minimum and include unstructured and semi structured information as well as formal systems.

Table 10 – Data asset list

Source	Owner	Store	Business process	Master reference data
GL	Finance	RDBMS	Accounts	Org structure, Accounts
Inventory	Ops	RDBMS	Orders, warehouse, distribution	Suppliers, Property, Products,
Training	Human Resources	Personal database	Training and staff development	Staff
Budgets	Finance	Spread sheet	Budgeting and forecasting	Products, Staff
Events	Marketing	Doc	Events management	Customers

A useful check is to compare the list of business processes in this table with the business processes identified in the process improvement strategy. If any you identified in the organisation chart are not present in the data asset list above, then you may have missed a repository. It is a sure bet that most office-based workers will be able to contribute to the list. However, you will probably be missing many of these personal data repositories in the first sweep.

This simple output is of value in its own right, but can also contribute towards a DW strategy. It may be the start of a discovery exercise for planning the data content of a DW[10].

Visibility and trust

Everyone who contributes to the list should be able to see the full results, saving exceptionally sensitive repositories. This is part of building a shared sense of trust and ownership of the data assets of the company. BI requires everyone in the business to contribute, but this sponsorship will only last as long as the advantages are obvious to all.

Even the seemingly innocuous task of creating a list of repositories may be controversial to some. An owner of a spreadsheet entitled *'Employee redundancy list – these guys have got to go!'* or, *'Top secret new products'* may have understandable reservations about publishing their existence to the whole company. My view is that we should still declare these data assets and publish their existence to those who have the requisite level of trust and authority in other business units or functions.

Neither should we shy away from publishing the existence of data assets that are normal business

---

[10] See *Recommended reading* Inmon (2005) and Kimball and Ross (2002) for more information on data warehouse planning and design

processes even though their content – which we are not publishing at this time – may be private or sensitive. Therefore, it follows that we should publish the existence of a spreadsheet that records employee remuneration or project outcomes.

A compelling reason for a bias in favour of visibility is that these sensitive repositories are also a treasure trove of master reference data. The remuneration review spreadsheet may be the only source in the company where we can find an employee's current qualifications and experience. Similarly, the project review spreadsheet may be the only accurate source of each project's duration and in fact the only place in the company where you can get a complete list of past projects. Although some of the data in the spreadsheet is sensitive, it also contains valuable master data that is not sensitive, and could be useful to other business processes. Raising the visibility of sensitive data sources creates an opportunity to share parts of the data whilst preserving the security of the sensitive elements.

Data quality

When a data quality issue arises, the obvious first step is to raise it with the source system owner. Ideally, they will clean up the mess in the source to resolve the problem; in reality, this may only fix a subset of the issues. For example, it may be a matter of urgency to correct customer addresses so that the invoices go to the right place. However, there will be far less incentive to look at historical transactions because they have no immediate impact on today's business.

Once you have exhausted the quick wins from tidying up at source, ETL tools can help cleanse the data automatically. You can apply business rules to fill missing values or create consistency. It is easy to obsess over data quality, but keep in mind that cleansing data is expensive and applying business rules too early can make it difficult for end users to reconcile back to source. You need to ask what level of quality is required for the intended application. For instance, if we need the average sales and transaction count per month for an EPOS (electronic point of sale) system in a supermarket, it is very unlikely that a few thousand bad transaction records over 5 years will have a material influence on our decision process. We return to the theme of continuous interaction between the BI specialist and the subject matter expert. This is the quickest route to judging the return on investment of an expensive data cleansing exercise.

It is great news if the data is one hundred per cent accurate, but in lieu of this nirvana, it is more important that the target users understand the degree of accuracy. They need to judge whether their decision process can tolerate the level of error. Different decisions processes will require different levels of confidence.

Security

Security requires a cultural solution rather than a technical one. It seems inevitable that more information, be it personal, technical, or political, will be in the public domain as time moves on. The music industry tried to swim against the tide by being too protective of their data. They appeared to be out of touch, and some companies have come close to going out of business.

Meanwhile search engine providers have published valuable proprietary information and services free of charge, whilst still earning huge revenues from other channels. Although, this might seem more a discussion on intellectual property than security, I think the two share similar qualities.

When I first specialised in BI, I found data protectionism to be more of an issue than it is today. Security can avoid embarrassment, maintain a monopoly on the provision of information (as with the music industry), or enforce a misplaced or politically motivated need-to-know culture. Denying access to data is easier than permitting it, especially if the benefits of sharing are not obvious.

Sharing data *is* riskier than not sharing it. The trick, as with any other business activity, is measuring the relative risks and benefits. The BI process-improvement strategy should highlight real benefits to sharing data. This tips the scales towards the benefits.

Business goals and security

One mechanism for removing security barriers starts with the organisation hierarchy and business goals that we discussed in Chapter 3. This high-level view is ideal for exposing goals that cross business units and functions. With this in mind, sharing data becomes a natural and mutually beneficial next step.

The culture of security is one that must filter down from the top of the organisation. If the boss is relaxed about close cooperation with other business units or functions, others will follow suit. Of course, the opposite applies if senior management foster a culture of protectionism.

Shared responsibility

A culture of openness requires everyone to be aware of the value of information. In the early days of email and the internet, companies invested a lot of effort educating staff on using these tools responsibly. A single misplaced email could do irrevocable damage to a company's reputation. The same is true for inappropriate web browsing, and yet these tools are now pervasive and business must accept the risk to remain competitive.

However, even here, discrepancies exist between different organisations that are indicative of the culture of trust. Some companies filter out webmail, social network sites, and job searching sites. Some allow them all. I have not observed a logical pattern to explain these discrepancies. Industries you might expect to have heightened security are often the most trusting and open.

You have to ask yourself, if users wanted to jeopardise the company, could they do so already with the data they currently use. If the answer is yes, then this alone should not be a reason for restricting access to data outside of their immediate responsibility.

Data source structure

There are several approaches to working with unstructured data.

Alternative source
It might seem a cop-out to say, find another source. However, it should be the first avenue to exhaust before considering expensive ETL. Unstructured content is often the presentation layer for more structured data. A webpage might retrieve data from a database. An invoice is just a formatted report of data in the operational system. In some cases, you will not be able to access the alternative source but it is worth checking nonetheless.

Request a different format
External entities are a common source of unstructured data. We may receive invoices from suppliers, bank

statements, industry survey results, all of which come in complex or apparently unstructured document formats. More often than not, these entities are happy and able to provide the data in a more structured format like CSV or XML. If you are one of their customers then they have a strong incentive to keep you happy. If *they* are the customer, then consider what additional information you could provide them and discuss a reciprocal agreement. In Chapter 1, we identified numerous benefits to providing our customers with BI solutions.

ETL and DW

ETL tools provide built in support for automatically parsing and extracting data from an array of different formats. Ideally, we should extract the data from the source format and load it into the DW. Once the data is stored in an RDBMS[11] then, irrespective of the data modelling approach, it should be much easier to work with and to share across the organisation.

Non-existing data

A DW is the best place to preserve data that would otherwise be lost with the passing of time. Unlike operational systems that frequently overwrite or delete data not required for current processes, we design DWs to store a history of data. We can take snapshots of volatile operational data and load them into the DW to capture a point-in-time record of attribute values.

If no operational systems capture the data, it may still exist in spreadsheets or documents. Again, we use the DW to store a snapshot of the artefact at regular intervals or in response to an event like the creation of a new

---

[11] RDBMS (relational database management system), see *Glossary*

document or change in an existing one. This may require some coordination with the process owner to ensure the documents have a defined structure and are located in an accessible area.

Update timing

If the data does not exist in the source system at the time we need it, then we can either look at alternative sources or streamline the process of updating the original system.

It may be impractical to update an operational system until after the time when we need the data. This is often the case where the information we need is just a by-product of recording another process in the system. In such cases, we should look upstream from the operational system. It is likely that the information is recorded elsewhere in a semi or unstructured format. If we can capture this data, we can load it into a DW, increasing the availability by faster publishing.

BI in practice

Dealing with delays in updating operational systems

A university system tracks the expenses related to laboratory experiments. It also records the outcome of the experiment. For operational efficiency the payments clerk does not add the experiment to the system until they have accounted for all the expenses. This can take several weeks.

We are interested in analysing recent trends in experiment effectiveness. The delay in updating the operational system had made previous analysis unreliable. We cannot convince the clerk to change their working practices so we request the lead scientist to copy us in on the email that first notifies the clerk about a completed experiment. The email contains a spreadsheet with information about the experiment. We can load the spreadsheet data into a DW and create timely analysis and reports.

The solution is ideal because it does not require any additional work from the clerk or the lead scientist. In early iterations, we want to prove the value of the BI approach before we burden others with additional work.

The solution also demonstrates the additional flexibility of having a DW to hold data that is not present in operational systems.

Data warehouse

DW is the most common method for increasing data availability. We use a DW to store and integrate data from other systems. Once the data is loaded into the DW, we typically keep it there for as long as it is required for analysis and decision support; this may be far longer than we would keep the data in the source systems.

The highly influential books[12], *Building the Data Warehouse*, by W.H. Inmon (Inmon, 2005), and *The Data Warehouse Toolkit: The Complete Guide to Dimensional Modelling*, by Ralph Kimball (Kimball and Ross, 2002), established and popularised DW as a formal methodology when they were first published in the 1990s. These texts provide a detailed explanation of the justifications for DW and practical advice on how to organise a DW project. There are some differences in emphasis between the two books but there is broad agreement on the advantages and purpose of a DW approach.

Data storage options

Before we look at the benefits of DW in more detail, it is worth briefly considering the alternatives. DW is not a prerequisite for BI and I have built many BI applications without using one. In the early days of your BI strategy, it is perfectly acceptable to develop BI solutions without following a strict DW methodology. In fact, if you wait until a DW is in place you may miss valuable opportunities to make quick wins. BI technology can often support simple business processes without the requirement for a high degree of data integration and

---

[12] See *Recommended reading*

availability. When we identify data that will be useful for BI, we have three basic choices:

1. Leave the data where it is and provide the technology, security, and information required to access it
2. Extract some or all of the data verbatim into a shared database repository (possibly the staging area of a DW)
3. Extract some or all of the data and integrate it with data from other repositories in a DW

Table 11 – Options for data storage and integration

Storage strategy	Relative initial cost	Data availability	Advantages
Source system	Low	Low-High depending on structure and system	Data is nearer real time and we reduce data storage costs by not duplicating it in a DW
Extract only	Low-Medium	Low-High depending on structure and system	Record a history of snapshots, and avoid security and load issues on source system

Storage strategy	Relative initial cost	Data availability	Advantages
Extract and integrate	High	High	Integration benefits many of the factors affecting availability (see Table 12 below)

The data strategy is likely to mature over time, moving from documentation, to a regular extraction, right through to full integration. We can use DW methods to identify, extract, and integrate data.

We have said that DW is not a prerequisite for BI development. Our primary concern is that the data is sufficiently available to use in the current BI project and that when we use it, we also increase the data availability for future projects. DW is a very good way to achieve these dual aims but not the only choice.

Data warehouse and data availability

The primary focus of this book is not DW and it is enough to discuss how DW contributes to data availability and look at some of the more critical decision points you may have when choosing to warehouse data. Table 12 (below) looks at some of the main benefits of DW and relates them to the availability factors we discussed earlier in the chapter.

Table 12 – Data warehouse contributions to data availability

Benefit	Data availability
Data integration	Integrating data from different source systems is time consuming and potentially complex. However, the process of integration usually increases the *data quality* by raising awareness of data issues and cleansing the data during ETL. Because the DW is a central source of data from different systems, this increases the *visibility* of the data throughout the organisation. If the DW holds integrated data, the BI project can concentrate on publishing the data to users. This reduces project costs and time-to-market
Query performance	Operational database design optimises record inserts, updates, and deletions. DW databases optimise query performance by using different physical and logical modelling strategies
Query availability compared to operational system	System administrators may impose restrictions on querying the operational data to avoid disruption to critical operational processes. A DW does need to support operational processes directly allowing us to run resource intensive queries

Benefit	Data availability
Historical data	An operational system may store a limited history of transaction data and then archive or delete old records to maintain performance. A DW will typically record a complete history of interesting transactions for historical analysis. An operational system may store only the current values of master data attributes like a company address or an employee's department. The DW can take snapshots of these values and store a history preventing loss of information as described in the *non-existing data* scenario
Derived data and custom groupings	Operational systems store the minimum information necessary for supporting operational processes. DWs can store whatever information is useful for analysis. For example, we may want to classify customers using our own grouping attributes, or analyse a product description field by extracting all the keywords into separate database fields. We can use the DW to capture any information that was previously *non-existing* in a structured format or data that is not captured early enough due to the *update timing* of the operational system
Unstructured data	A DW can be a central repository for data that is useful but not stored in core operational systems. Examples include spreadsheet data; flat files from suppliers, customers, or other third parties; and log files. The ETL process may improve the *data structure* and integrity of the data, raising the availability to other applications

Data warehouse modelling

DW data modelling is a technical subject and we cover it very briefly in this section. If you are a non-technical reader, you may find the following discussion a bit dry. If so, please move to the subsequent sections on ETL, data ownership, and business rules, which return to a more business oriented perspective.

3NF and dimensional modelling are the two main approaches to modelling data in the DW. We normally implement a DW using an RDBMS and we can use either modelling approach in this environment.

3NF data modelling

3NF modelling is the approach used in most operational systems but is also used for some DW. A relational data model consisting of tables, columns, and relationships is in the 3NF if it adheres to a set of rules designed to avoid data duplication and integrity issues. 3NF modelling is a very good way of maintaining data integrity. The constraints also provide a level of self-documentation about the meaning of the data that can be lost using dimensional modelling.

There are two perceived disadvantages of using a 3NF data model for the DW. Firstly, it is difficult for non-technical users to understand the data model and write queries directly against it. Secondly, because of the data model complexity, we normally have to create dimensional models in additional to the 3NF model to support analysis and BI tools. This means that a DW in 3NF will probably be more expensive to implement than a dimensional DW.

Dimensional modelling

The second approach to DW modelling is dimensional modelling. A dimensional model does not enforce data integrity to the same extent as 3NF. However, the model is much better suited to analysis because it is more intuitive to users and equivalent queries execute much faster. Many analytical databases and end user tools anticipate a dimensional model.

We can construct a dimensional model from queries on a 3NF database or materialise the structure in the DW. In common with 3NF models, it is not a prerequisite of BI applications that you implement a dimensional model. The driving factor is the extent to which the chosen model increases data availability – by lowering the cost of acquisition – for the intended purpose.

Guidance on choosing a modelling approach

You do not need to choose a single modelling approach for the entire DW. In practice, you will probably model different data sources using different approaches depending on your goal.

If the DW has to integrate and maintain data from a variety of complex structured and unstructured sources then you will probably want to validate the integrity of the integrated data. The process of integration is effectively creating a repository of original data and the same considerations apply as if you were maintaining the data for operational purposes. A 3NF model is a proven method of maintaining data integrity.

If you are confident about the integrity of the source system data, do not have much data integration, and have a specific purpose in mind then a dimensional modelling approach will probably be quicker and less costly than creating a 3NF DW model.

There is plenty of information about the relative merits of the two approaches. I recommend that those wanting a deeper understanding read *both* Imhoff (2003) and Kimball (2002).[13]

Modelling time in the warehouse

One of the great benefits of a DW is the ability to track and record changes in data over time. For instance, if we wanted to look at the effect of product packaging on sales, it is interesting to know that a particular product had red packaging in year 1, and blue packaging in year 2. The history of package information may not be available in the original source system – it may only record the current colour of the packaging. Using a DW, we can capture the package colour and record a history of changes.

When business users think about examples like the one above, their first impulse is to request that we track the history of changes for all their reference data. We should strongly resist this impulse because accurately modelling changing data is conceptually complex (see Malinowski, E. & Zimányi, E. (2006))[14], validating it is resource intensive, and interpreting the results is, in my experience, the most frequent cause of confusion for users and developers of the DW. In any given scenario, a user can describe exactly how they would expect a change in attribute value to be treated. Unfortunately, each new scenario leads to a different expectation.

---

[13] See *Recommended reading*
[14] See *Recommended reading*

It helps to consider the reality of operational processes before deciding whether to record the history of an attribute in the DW. Data entry mistakes, delays in updating databases, and backdated corrections can all frustrate our ability to record history correctly. When we integrate data from different sources, each updated at different frequencies, it is even more difficult to appreciate the real meaning of the resulting data.

Put simply, if we record the history of an attribute in a DW we make a statement about our ability to record it accurately. Users may not be sympathetic to the nuances of the underlying operational process that render our history inaccurate.

BI in practice

Historical attribute values in the DW

A company uses a DW to integrate data from two systems. The first is a billing system that records invoices and payments. The second is a CRM system that records the current holding company and industry sector for each customer.

We can relate records from the billing system with records from the CRM system using a customer identifier. This allows us to analyse billings by holding company and industry type over time.

The company updates the billing system every day with new invoices and receipts. The DW ETL process extracts the new records from the billing system each night. The nightly process also takes a snapshot of the CRM attributes, building a history of changes to the holding company and industry sector of each customer. The tables below show

how the history of CRM attribute changes might look in the DW.

----- *Holding company history table (CRM data source)*

Customer	Holding Co.	Start Date	End Date
10021	Small Corp	21-Mar-09	29-Jun-10
10021	Big Corp	30-Jun-10	

----- *Industry sector history table (CRM data source)*

Customer	Sector	Start Date	End Date
10021	Courier	01-Feb-08	25-Jan-10
10021	Freight	26-Jan-10	

The following table shows a single record from the billing history table

----- *Billing history table (Billing data source)*

Customer Id	Invoice No.	Amount	Inv. Date
10021	301	$3,000	15-Jan-10

Based on the invoice date and the CRM information in the DW, we can allocate the invoice for $3,000 to the Small Corp holding company and the Courier industry sector.

Unfortunately, what is invisible to the DW user is that the company only updates the CRM system periodically, when a sales representative meets with a customer. At this point, the sales representative asks the customer for their latest details and records them in the CRM system. The Start Date and End Date recorded in the DW represent the update time in the CRM system, not when the event occurred in the real world.

Let us say that customer *10021* changed holding company and industry sector on the 15-Dec-09. The sales representative meets with the customer on the 25-Jan-10.

After this meeting, the sales representative updates the industry sector but forgets about the holding company. It is only at the second meeting, on 29-Jun-10, that they update the holding company.

The realities of the operational process thwart our attempts to accurately record history in the DW. Operational processes can also change over time, subtly changing the semantics of the DW data. Even if we understand the sales representative's business process and update timings, it does not necessarily mean that the process was always this way, or that it will be so in the future.

The example is worth remembering because it is so common. There are a number of possible solutions for creating a more accurate history, or making the meaning of the history tables clearer, but they all involve additional cost. If we are selective about the historical information we record, we have a far better chance of correctly representing the real world in the DW.

Extract, transform, and load (ETL)

ETL is the term used to describe taking data from the source system (EXTRACT); data cleansing, integration, and applying business rules (TRANSFORM); and moving it into the final destination – often a DW (LOAD). An array of specialist tools exists to help with every aspect of this process.

One of the inconvenient truths of DW and BI is that you can easily spend far more time analysing data quality, cleansing data, and moving data around, than developing the end user interaction layer that will provide the real value to the business processes. This can be a source of great frustration for many BI specialists, who would rather be getting to grips with the business problems and creating the end user deliverables than writing ETL procedures.

A certain amount of data manipulation is essential to provide the users with quality integrated data and apply business rules. A successful ETL project that integrates and cleanses frequently used data will drastically reduce the cost of developing subsequent BI solutions that use the same data. These potential gains must be balanced by the fact that ETL is expensive, time consuming and error prone; so you need to be sure of the return on investment before you do any more than is required for the immediate purpose.

The most effective method of containing ETL spend is for the BI specialist to speak directly with the subject matter expert. From these discussions, it should become apparent which data sources will contribute most to supporting the business process.

It is likely that some of the data will be difficult and expensive to integrate. This may not be an issue if the user can retrieve it efficiently using the existing process. Do not assume that just because the data is difficult to extract that it is pivotal to supporting the business process.

BI in practice

Practical compromises on data integration

An events manager organises a weekly social evening. The company is an IT consultancy and the event provides an informal setting for the consultants to meet with clients that have recently started a new project, or finished an existing one.

The manager wants a BI solution to support the process by providing details of customers with relevant projects (recently started or finished), consultants' diaries for availability, and information to help determine the venue.

The events manager identifies the following data sources:

```
HR database containing staff diary information

CRM database for client contacts and emails

Billing system for project initiation and billing

Websites of venues

Website and web service for weather information
```

The manager has noticed that outdoor events have better attendance, so he uses weather data to determine if an outdoor venue is practical. Ideally, he would like venue information and weather data integrated into the solution. However, it transpires that due to firewall restrictions and complexities with the venue and weather websites, it will be expensive and time consuming to integrate this data.

The other systems are less problematic and so the solution will automatically identify potential clients, match them with staff availability and suggest the day with the greatest potential attendance of clients and staff. From that point, the manager will continue the manual effort of browsing the weather and venue websites to complete the process.

Although not a perfect solution, the manager spent the majority of time identifying projects, clients, and staff availability. Now that we have supported this process, the manager has more time to select the right venue, albeit by continuing with their original process.

Data ownership

If we do not feel in control of the data we need, our natural response is to create our own version of it. This can be anything from an individual user creating a spreadsheet to a department procuring a system. Acknowledging this truth will ensure we do not jeopardise the data strategy by making it appear like a big brother exercise to control all the data in the organisation. The data strategy is not about data ownership. The owners of the data should continue to own it. We have to accept that they are free to make last minute corrections, updates, or introduce complications, however inconvenient this might be for data availability. We can gently encourage data owners to provide some support for the process, but in the early stages of the BI program, when the benefits of data sharing and availability are unproven, we should not overplay our hand.

If a user group suspect a threat to their ownership of the data through the imposition of rules and service levels, then one of two negative things may happen. Firstly, they may reduce our ability to use the data by only sharing the data once it is completely stable in the system. Secondly, if enough pressure is applied, they may fully share their data, but take the business processes underground into spreadsheets and personal databases, only updating the source system when the process is all but over.

If we are concerned about the consistency of the data, we can introduce reporting and auditing to pick up unanticipated changes. When the BI strategy emerges with real deliverables and the data owners can see the benefits then there is an opportunity to request more assistance. At the start of the BI data strategy, we should treat data owners with kid gloves, respecting their ownership of the data.

The great spreadsheet explosion debate

One of the first things you may read in BI and DW literature is that these methods should help rein in the proliferation of spreadsheets. Certainly, we hope to provide alternatives to manual data manipulation and reporting in spreadsheets. However, spreadsheets are popular for a reason. They are easy to work with, modify, and have powerful built in features. Most importantly, users feel in control of the data in their personal spreadsheets.

I would not judge the success of a BI project by the reduction in the number of actively used spreadsheets in the organisation. Rather than focus on the more abstract goal of reducing spreadsheet use, let us first review the objectives of users and the wider BI strategy in relation to spreadsheets.

Spreadsheets are popular because they:

- ✓ allow the owner to have complete control of the data
- ✓ have powerful tools for analysing the data
- ✓ often have the most up-to-date version of the business process data

However, spreadsheets:

- ▪ can be an inefficient method of repetitive data integration and manipulation
- ▪ are not a stable or integral way to store data
- ▪ are not a very effective way of sharing data

Spreadsheets are often a midway step to completing a business process before entering the final value in the

ERP/operational system. This is generally because the operational system only records the outcome of the process rather than supporting it.

BI methods can reduce the amount of work performed in spreadsheets but we must tackle one process at a time. The following section looks at some practical techniques for managing spreadsheets globally. With these simple steps, we move towards viewing them as a shared asset rather than a liability.

Tactics for spreadsheet management
Over the last 10 years, I have observed BI vendors swing from actively marketing alternatives to spreadsheets, back to actively encouraging their use. I think we can safely assume that spreadsheet use will only increase over time. There are practical – and perhaps obvious – steps we can take to manage our increasing reliance on spreadsheets. These should help reduce inefficiency and risk in our business.

Step 1 – Shared network drive or portal for all routine spreadsheets
To reduce the risk of data loss and provide greater visibility we should save all routine process-oriented spreadsheets to a shared area with a regular backup routine.

Step 2 – Regular upload to warehouse
Where a spreadsheet contains primary data[15] not stored in other repositories, or where there is a significant delay in it being available in other repositories, we should discuss the merits of making it available in the DW. This can give immediate benefits to the owner through access to

---

[15] Primary data – data that is first created or recorded in the repository as opposed to being taken from another source

versions of the data, and provide additional visibility of the primary data to other users who may be interested in it.

The spreadsheet may be as simple as a list of the day's exchange rates. We may currently distribute it via email. Once the data is in the DW, it is easier for us to integrate it into new reports.

If the spreadsheet is quite unstructured, you may have to work with the owner to improve the structure of the useful data before scheduling a load.

Step 3 – Spreadsheet database query tool

A growing number of BI tools allow you to interact with databases directly from spreadsheets. Some of these tools can maintain live links to the data in the database whilst others create point in time exports into the spreadsheet environment.

Step 4 – Automate redundant data integration

Some spreadsheets are simply a collation of data from other sources and have no primary data. These are candidates for automation using BI tools. With Steps 1-3 in place, it may be easier to automate the creation of the spreadsheet content from data in the DW. The *BI in practice* example below is one such scenario.

Conclusion

With these four simple steps, we have significantly reduced the inherent risks and disadvantages of spreadsheet use. At the same time, we have increased data availability and encouraged users to start using the BI tools to collate their data.

Importantly, the users still have complete control of their data. In the end, we should reduce the number of relationships between spreadsheets as people move towards sourcing their data directly from the DW and related databases.

BI in practice

Automating data acquisition whilst maintaining ownership

Each morning a marketing manager records the share price and relevant stories about the company's clients in a spreadsheet.

After some collaborative research with a BI specialist they realise the data is available via a web service. The BI specialist writes an ETL process to extract the data from the web service and save it to a database.

The manager uses the time saved by the ETL process to analyse the data and deliver market insights. The manager continues to own and control the data but the information is now more available, easier to manipulate, and the manager is able to focus on their primary business objectives.

Business rules

Business rules are worth considering in isolation because they are a frequent cause of frustration when implementing BI. The question that we must consider is, when and where should we define business rules in the BI solution?

The answer is dependent on the stability of the business rule (whether it changes frequently or is reasonable static) and how widely accepted the business rule is within the organisation as a whole.

The mythical one version of the truth

"When I use a word,' Humpty Dumpty said in rather a scornful tone, 'it means just what I choose it to mean — neither more nor less." Through the Looking-Glass, and What Alice Found There – Lewis Carroll

One of the greatest myths pervading BI is that there is one version of the truth within an organisation, just waiting to be found. Ask any senior manager whether there should be one version of the truth and they will immediately agree, citing numerous frustrations caused by the lack of uniformity. Many a time in my days as an analyst did I wish for one version of the truth when I produced a report and was told it was incorrect because the revenue figure in the report did not agree with the revenue figure in another report. However, when I looked into the discrepancies between two apparently similar reports there were good reasons for the differences. The reports had different audiences with a different objective.

One possible solution is to create a standard set of names for measures and other commonly used attributes. So *sales* might breakdown into: *financial accounts sales; management accounts sales; sales for the purposes of assessing sales rep performance (excluding rebates and indirect commercial discounts); sales reported to industry survey provider (according to their rules at the time); sales for the purposes of billing a customer on a long term agreement; sales for the purpose of billing a customer with a volume rebate.*

An organisation may have hundreds of these measures and attributes, each having many derivatives with slightly different nuances. Just compiling and agreeing on a shortlist is a stressful exercise. Maintaining the list is difficult and using them in practice is more complex still. For the sake of report presentation, it is impractical to augment every label in a report or dashboard with a full and unequivocal name.

Perhaps the biggest issue is that the one version of the truth can shift over time due to regulatory changes, new industry practices, or management personnel changes. If you are storing historical data in your DW, do you report historical figures according to the old truth or new truth?

When a person speaks of one version of the truth, the best we can normally say is that it represents the truth as they see it at the current point in time. Striving for one version of the truth, even if it is a point-in-time version, is a worthy objective. However, we should not place too much reliance on the stability of the truth when we implement it as business rules in our data strategy.

Applying business rules

The previous section sets the scene for a pragmatic approach to applying business rules in the data strategy.

BI in practice

Applying business rules too early

A company requires a daily snapshot of the number of employees in the organisation. Everyone agrees that an employee is someone who works part time or full time, but contractors, and those on maternity leave should not be included in the count.

The payroll system has a flag to differentiate the employment types. If an employee's status changes from contractor to part time, the system overwrites the current value with the new one. The daily extract provides a snapshot of the number of employees with the relevant flag value for each day.

For a couple of years the company extracts a count of all the employees that are full time or part time on that day. A change in government regulation means the company must now treat those on maternity leave as employees for reporting purposes so they change the daily extract logic to include them.

The history of daily count figures now represents two different calculated values. We cannot go back and recover a history of employees who were on maternity leave because the system only records a point in time status value. Equally, historical trends are difficult to interpret because an awareness of the change in business rules is required.

In this scenario, the problem occurs because the data is summarised and filtered before it reaches the DW. This is not good practice and an experienced practitioner would probably avoid it.

Nonetheless, we could have a similar situation where we extracted all the employee records, but then applied a business rule to the employee status to update all employees that are not full time or part time to 'Non-employees'. In this instance, we have done the right thing by extracting the detailed data, but still lost the history of the employee category by applying a categorisation business rule to the column and not preserving the original data.

Figure 12 (below) shows a simplified version of the generic BI solution architecture (see *Chapter 5 – Technology strategy*, for more detail) with guidance on where to implement business rules.

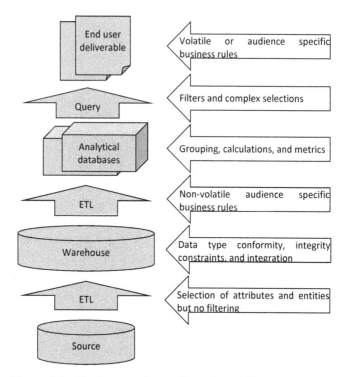

Figure 12 – Business rules enforced at different levels of the architecture

There is an obvious trade off in the placement of business rules. The closer to the source system the rule is enforced, (towards the bottom of the architecture diagram above) the greater the chance of consistency across your reporting and analysis. On the other hand, if the business rule changes or becomes inapplicable to some parts of your reporting and analysis, the cost of changing the rule is far greater if it resides in a layer with a number of dependent layers above it. As a rule, it is far cheaper and easier to adjust calculations or groupings enforced in a couple of reports or an analytical database, than it is to make the same changes in the ETL or DW because of the chain of dependencies.

At the DW layer, my preference is to avoid filters, groupings, and categorisations that overwrite source system classifications. It should be possible to query the DW and reconcile the results back to the source system without having to perform acrobatics with the data. This is a very important part of user acceptance especially in the early stages of a BI project. If users do not trust the data, they will continue to use their own methods to extract it.

Analytical databases are ideal for applying filters, custom groupings, calculations, and algorithms. They have a more expressive query language than standard SQL, and because they are not the permanent historical data store, there is less impact if you have to rebuild them. You should probably expect to build a number of analytical databases for different objectives; each one can apply department or business unit specific logic.

Some practitioners have a strong objection to putting business logic in the reporting layer citing inconsistency and maintenance issues if the calculation logic changes. There is truth here, but I think it is over emphasised for various reasons. Firstly, it assumes that there will not be a maintenance issue in the dependent reports if the business rule resides in the database, which is not the case (see *BI in practice* example, below). Secondly, most reports have a far shorter *useful* lifespan than their actual lifespan. Recipients often cancel or significantly modify reports when they require maintenance. Finally, the argument assumes that the cost of putting all business logic in a database – be it relational or analytical – is significantly lower. Most reports belong to a small number of users who should know and be able to validate the business logic. If we were to squeeze all the business logic in all the reports of any organisation into a single database, the result would be thousands of lines of code that unless fastidiously maintained, would soon become impenetrable. When reports lack traceability users tend to go back to the source for their enquiries.

BI in practice

Calculation logic implicitly embedded in a report format

An analytical database for a department store defines the following calculation:

Revenue = Sales + Rental Income (from subleasing shop space)

Here is the format for one of their reports that uses the calculated revenue figure and then reports rebates and other discounts as separate items:

```
Revenue:                        4000.00
Less
Rebate:                         1000.00
Discounts:                       500.00
Revenue less discounts:         2500.00
```

They decide to modify the calculation of revenue to include rebates.

Revenue = Sales + Rental Income – Rebates

They adjust the calculation in the database. They also adjust the dependent calculation: *Revenue less discounts.*

However, the report format has not changed and still anticipates rebates as a separate line item. The report looks inconsistent now that rebates are part of revenue.

```
Revenue:                        3000.00
Less
Rebate:                         1000.00
Discounts:                      500.00
Revenue less discounts:         2500.00
```

Although the calculations for each individual value in the report are correct, they still need to modify the report to make the report layout consistent with the data.

The modified version of the report format (below) removes the rebates as a separate line item because it is now included as part of the revenue calculation.

```
Revenue:                        3000.00
Less
Discounts:                      500.00
Revenue less discounts:         2500.00
```

Summary

In this chapter, we discussed the essential elements of the data strategy in more detail. We covered:

- ✓ Factors that influence the availability of data to BI solutions
- ✓ Promoting data availability in the organisation
- ✓ DW and the impact of different storage options on data availability
- ✓ Differences between data ownership and the data strategy and some practical advice for managing spreadsheets
- ✓ ETL
- ✓ Business rules and *one version of the truth*

The key messages from the chapter are:

- ❖ The data strategy is a continuous commitment to improving the visibility and availability of data in the organisation
- ❖ We should understand the various factors that influence data availability because they have such a strong influence on the cost and integrity of BI solutions
- ❖ The first steps towards promoting data availability should provide quick wins at low expense. Publishing an inventory of data sources is a good place to start. Promoting a culture that favours responsible data sharing between business units and departments is also effective
- ❖ Do not expect data source owners to jump through hoops to clean up their data in the early stages of a BI program. We must gain sponsorship by delivering value to the business

- ❖ Be pragmatic about the level of data quality required. 100% data quality and consistency is very difficult to achieve and is not necessary for many applications of BI
- ❖ DW is still the best long term approach for raising data availability although it is not a prerequisite for developing BI solutions
- ❖ Data integration and tracking changes in master data over time can give rise to a number of subtle issues in the DW that affect the meaning of the data. Technical solutions and modelling techniques alone, will not necessarily resolve these
- ❖ Many business rules are volatile or specific to a particular department or business unit. If we want to share data, we should not apply business rules too early in the BI solution architecture
- ❖ Creating one version of the truth seems desirable but is not always practical because of the varied objectives and perspectives in the business as well as changes to the business environment over time. Aim for clarity of meaning in end-user deliverables but do not be too concerned about creating a universal statement of truth

5.   Technology strategy

Introduction to the technology strategy

Let us recap why BI offers such potential.

> BI **technology** *enables a solution to be realised at a non-prohibitive cost and in a short timeframe. Using specialist software in the right way is what makes successful BI projects so productive.*

Each BI project will only provide maximum return on investment if the path from conception to implementation is short and efficient. The BI tools are the vehicle for this journey and the core components must be in place early in the BI strategy. The technology pillar of the BI strategy must:

1. Provide the infrastructure and tools to support common BI solutions
2. Educate the organisation on the different capabilities of each tool so they can correctly match the problem with the technology solution

The technology strategy guides you through the minefield of BI tool selection. If you are not an IT manager, you may be tempted to skip this chapter. Please read on. It is important for everyone to understand the purpose of each component in the generic BI solution architecture and the value it offers to the business.

What do we cover in this chapter?

We start the chapter with some principles that should guide us when we first initiate the technology strategy. Next, we identify the components of the generic BI solution architecture. These fall broadly into two categories. Firstly, the data storage components used to implement the data strategy and increase data availability. Secondly, the user interaction components through which we deliver BI insights and value to the business. We consider each in turn and discuss appropriate applications of the technology and common limitations. Having gained an appreciation of the capabilities of each component, we then look at the process of procuring BI tools. We discuss the different types of BI vendors and look at common criteria for tool selection. We finish the chapter with some practical advice on building a hardware infrastructure and environment management.

Guiding principles of the technology strategy

The goal of the BI technology strategy is to provide the infrastructure and support for the BI tools that will deliver the data and process improvement pillars of the BI strategy. Careful tool selection will save time and money and ensure you have properly covered off the main categories of BI capability without unnecessary duplication.

As with the process and data strategy, we should not attempt to implement the technology strategy in one big bang. Although it is very tempting to *tick the box*, this is most likely to incur significant expense, raising expectations that we cannot possibly match by business productivity improvements in the short to medium term.

Several principles should guide our thinking in the early days of implementing our technology strategy.

1. Do not immediately sign up for an all-singing-all-dancing BI suite. Either get a long-term evaluation licence or cherry pick inexpensive BI components from different vendors. You need to have experience in several real BI projects before you can say which products will work within your organisation

2. Start with just a single environment capable of hosting development work and some early production ready solutions

3. Where possible, use licences and tools already available within the organisation. This is particularly the case with database management software and ETL tools

4. Accept that different user groups will want different user facing BI tools and do not put all your eggs (money) in one basket (vendor's pocket)

5. The technology strategy should also consider non-functional requirements like availability, security, and performance but this should not be the primary concern in the early stages. Instead, use one or two well-specified off-the-shelf servers and go from there

Most importantly, the BI technology strategy should make the tools and infrastructure readily available to any business unit, power user, or developer who has an idea for improving a business process. This is no time for protectionism, especially in the early stages of the technology strategy. We must allow users to experiment and take controlled risks.

Business intelligence solution architecture

Although there are a very large number of BI tools on the market, they broadly fall within just a few functional categories. Figure 13 (below) represents each category as a component of the generic BI solution architecture. Most common BI problems are solved with a combination of these components all doing what they do best. This is the most effective way to build a BI application, playing each tool to its strengths. We can waste time and resources if we ask a single tool to play outside of its core competency.

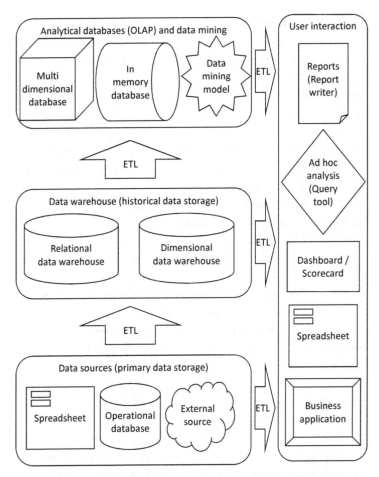

Figure 13 – Generic BI solution architecture

Looking at the diagram above, your first response might be why do I need all this stuff? At first, it seems like a lot of moving parts. However, just like more familiar home-office software, each tool has a distinct purpose that is not easy to replicate using other components. By example, although it is possible to write a letter in a spreadsheet application, there are many good reasons why it is better to use a word processing application.

The diagram has two main segments. On the left of the figure is the data storage architecture. This typically includes three tiers: primary data sources, a DW, and analytical databases. On the right of the figure are the end user tools. We can use an existing application as the interface for BI information – ideal for supporting a business process – or use specialist query tools, reports, dashboards, and spreadsheets.

The diagram illustrates two important features of the generic BI solution architecture.

1. The BI user interaction tools can legitimately interact with data from any layer in the data architecture

2. A mature BI technology capability will support a variety of end user tools

The second point may surprise some readers who would imagine that consolidating BI tools should be a driving force of a technology strategy. Consolidation is desirable for the DW, ETL, and (to a lesser extent) analytical databases. The user community for these development tools is relatively homogeneous – power users and technology professionals. In contrast, the preferred style of interaction for end user tools is much more subjective with different user groups favouring different tools.

The solution architecture diagram covers the broad categories of user interaction. Within each category, you will find many distinct products that provide the functionality in different ways. As a starting point, you should aim to provide a tool for each of these categories. As new user groups and requirements come on board, you should be open to incorporating new tools.

Justifications for expanding the end user toolset are that the new tool:

- is particularly well suited to supporting a business process or user group
- does not simply replicate a subset of functionality provided by an existing tool
- can be justified in terms of upfront cost and ongoing maintenance versus expected benefit

Many user-facing tools in the BI space are quite inexpensive or come free with other software and are easy to implement on a single desktop PC. In this instance, the threshold for justification should be quite low if a business user feels that it will support their process better than existing tools. Where a new tool is expensive and requires its own server infrastructure and dedicated support, we would expect a more rigorous approval process.

We now consider each of the components of the generic BI solution architecture in more detail.

Data storage architecture

You will typically require three layers of accessible data storage for your BI solutions: primary data storage; DW/historical storage; and analytical databases. In addition, you will require an ETL tool to move data between each of the layers.

Data sources (primary data storage)

The first layer is comprised of source systems that hold the primary data. I use the term *primary data* to emphasise that the systems are the original source of the data rather than being comprised of data collected from other systems. Examples might include ERP systems, semi structured data like spreadsheets or other documents, and external sources like web services or subscriptions.

Where the BI solution requires near-real-time data you may point your BI user tools and applications (Figure 13, right) directly at these primary data sources.

In addition to real-time capability, an advantage of using the source systems directly is that you do not have to replicate the data to a DW, which can be time consuming. Of course, a DW has many advantages that you do not get with this approach.

The technology strategy should identify appropriate tools to extract data from these data sources. We should also provide guidance as to when it is appropriate to move data directly from the source system to the end user tool, and when it should be via the DW layer.

Data warehouse (historical data storage)

In the previous chapter on data strategy, we discussed the reasons for building a DW. Here we look at the technology requirements to support this functionality.

The persistent historical storage layer should be supported by a server based (as opposed to personal) RDBMS. If *immediate* requirements envisage many terabytes of data, then you may consider specialist DW software or even a *data warehouse appliance*[16].

However, I cannot imagine recommending that an organisation with a new or immature BI strategy start by implementing these specialist products. It would be the equivalent of buying a Formula 1 racing car for driving lessons. Even if you have many terabytes of data, you

---

[16] Data warehouse appliance, see *Glossary*

should initially consider building your BI capability with the organisation's existing RDBMS software and less ambitious goals. After a few short projects, you will be in a much better position to know the exact challenges you need to address.

For the vast majority of BI projects, an off the shelf standard RDBMS is sufficient. In the previous chapter, we briefly discussed the differences between 3NF DW modelling and dimensional modelling. In either case, we would use a RDBMS.

BI user tools often query analytical data stores and do not interact directly with the RDBMS DW layer. This leads to the question: why do I have this redundant storage, why not store the historical data in the analytical database? RDBMS have a number of features that are unavailable or poorly supported in analytical databases. These include:

- Data constraints including referential integrity, uniqueness, and complex data types
- Fine grained control over updating and amending data to support backdated corrections, amendments and incremental loads
- Standard SQL interface for querying, manipulating and extracting data
- Logging, backup scheduling, and failover
- Scalability management

This functionality is essential for the ongoing maintenance of the DW.

Analytical databases (OLAP)

Analytical databases (OLAP) come in a number of styles but they share three common attributes:

- they are designed and optimised for efficient querying
- they make it easier and more intuitive for the user to interact directly with the data model for ad hoc analysis
- they provide a simpler and more powerful expression language for defining typical analytical calculations

Analytical databases provide faster and more flexible query analysis than can be achieved through an RDBMS with equivalent hardware. They are able to do this because the data model is not concerned with supporting the ongoing maintenance and integrity of the data. Analytical databases are one of the most exciting areas of BI with the latest products able to consume huge quantities of data whilst maintaining very fast query response times. For this reason, they are well suited for ad hoc query or interactive dashboards and reports.

Logical data model

The logical data model for an analytical database typically stores more information (metadata) about the data than a relational model. For instance, it may store the display order for a series of attributes. A simple example is the days of the week. Rather than displaying them in alphabetical order, we may specify the sort order as Monday, Tuesday, Wednesday…Sunday. This additional information increases the usability of the data model for ad hoc analysis.

Many databases use a multidimensional data model comprised of dimensions (representing things like customers and products) and fact tables (representing transactions and events like sales). Some data models make no logical distinction between master data and transaction data, and allow *slice and dice* on any attribute in the database.

Physical data model and performance

Most analytical databases store at least part of the data in memory; compile and manage frequently requested queries and data aggregations; and implement a highly compressed and indexed physical data model. These factors all contribute to the exceptional query response times that analytical databases provide.

It is worth noting that complex data models and algorithmic calculations can have a detrimental impact on query performance. It would be a mistake to assume that just because a vendor demonstration showed sub-second query response time on 100 GB of data, that the same query performance will be possible when your business rules and algorithms are applied to the model, even if you have significantly less data.

Query language

Another common attribute of analytical databases is an expressive query language better suited to typical analytical queries than SQL. One popular query language is MDX[17]. It exploits the additional metadata stored in a multidimensional data model. Even simple MDX calculations can provide answers to business questions

---

[17] See *Recommended reading*, Spofford (2006) for more information on MDX

that would traditionally have required a SQL programmer.

MDX is not the only query language available for analytical databases. Most either support this standard or their own bespoke language. Generally, the language makes it straightforward to define calculations including:

- Time trend analysis
- Ratios at different levels of aggregation
- Set definition and manipulation

A typical question for an analytical database might be:

For each of my ten most popular products this year by volume in each region, with decreasing volume over the last three years: show me the sales and margin for the current year by period and the top sales rep for each of the products in the period and their percentage contribution to the sales.

Table 13 – Result set from an analytical database query

Pro-duct	Re-gion	Sales Rep	Per-iod	Sales	Mar-gin	Sales Rep %
Com-puter	North	Janet Jones	Jan	100K	10%	30%
Prin-ter	North	Henry House	Jan	30K	15%	20%
Scan-ner	South	Toby Talbot	Jan	25K	25%	40%
Mouse	South	Prue Percy	Jan	130K	30%	5%

One interesting feature of such a query is that the selection criteria for the list of products are independent of the information we wish to report. This type of question would require a lot of SQL code and take a long time to execute on a SQL RDBMS. In contrast, we could express the same query with just a few lines of MDX and expect it to return results much more rapidly than the equivalent SQL query.

Query interface

One shortcoming of some analytical databases is that they lack a standard query interface. If the database supports a standard language like MDX then you should be able to query it with any compatible tool. This gives you more flexibility to embed queries within your business applications. A large number of analytical databases have a tightly coupled database and user interface. If the database is proprietary with no published query interface it may be difficult to query the database using anything other than the vendors own tools.

Data mining models

The traditional pattern of analysis normally starts with a hypothesis. For instance, we might hypothesise that the location of a customer influences how quickly they pay their invoices. We then ask questions to prove or disprove the hypothesis.

Are my international customers better at paying their invoices than domestic customers?

We perform the analysis ending with a conclusion that either supports or refutes that hypothesis. Data-mining questions are more open ended. You might ask questions like:

What products should I be marketing to which customers?

What are the key factors that determine the success of a new shop?

There are a number of data mining algorithms, each best suited to particular questions and outputs. Data mining is not an entry-level BI project. It requires a good knowledge of the data, an appreciation of data mining algorithms, and a deep understanding of the business domain to identify interesting patterns.

Advocates of data mining emphasise that the preparation work can be as informative as the process of running the algorithm. A mining algorithm can make hundreds of passes over the data set so it is important that the data is clean and that the structure is suitable for machine processing.

BI in practice

Analysing the results of data mining

A company provides travel consultancy to organisations around the world. They book flights and hotels and charge a commission for the service. They collect information about their customers and want to use this to understand more about them.

The first thing they want to know is what makes for a profitable customer. If they can understand the commonalities of profitable customers, they can concentrate their resources on marketing to those customers.

They run a mining algorithm on all the attributes that they have collected about the customer. The result tells them that the most significant contributors to profitability are customers with high revenue and high margin. Well that is undeniably true but ultimately unhelpful as it only asserts a mathematical relationship between margin, revenue, and profit.

However, the results also reveal that long-term customers based in city centres with a presence in Asia are a high predictor of profitability. This leads to further questions and analysis but also reveals potential opportunities. For instance, they may want to target similar companies who are not existing customers.

One of the questions we should always ask is whether we have really found the predictive attributes or a side effect of an attribute outside of the data we have analysed.

In our present scenario, further analysis reveals that the company's top sales manager manages all the customers in the high profitability group. So are the customers highly profitable because they are long-term city based customers with a presence in Asia, or, is it because the highflying sales manager manages them? Is the sales manager's performance attributable to hard work and natural talent or are they just lucky enough to be managing the long-term customers with a presence in Asia?

In my experience, data mining is not as popular as reports and dashboards. The results of a data mining exercise are hard to predict and it is even harder to find specialists in data mining. However, there are plenty of applications of data mining that are intuitive to business people and do not require a huge investment.

The most commonly cited application of data mining is market basket analysis. Larger retailers have used this technique for many years. Market basket analysis finds relationships between collections of items that would be difficult to detect using more manual analysis techniques. The basket is the shopping basket or cart and the analysis finds the likelihood of different collections of items appearing together in a shopping cart.

It may be obvious to everyone that if a person buys a tennis racket, that same person is more likely to buy tennis balls. Market basket analysis can provide insight into subtle relationships between items that are not so intuitive. For instance, we might find that if a parent buys children's football boots they also buy a doll or toy car; the rationale being that if one child gets football boots the other child should also get a present. This understanding can help us with cross selling, promotions, and product placement in the store.

Extract, transform, and load (ETL)

The technology strategy should specify the tools for moving data between the different storage layers to make it more available for end user applications. You should definitely use a specialist ETL tool for this purpose.

ETL tools can perform an array of functions including data profiling to determine data quality, advanced data manipulation and transformations, job scheduling, data load management, exception handling, logging, and workflow. Typically, ETL tools automate many of the routine steps in ETL development and provide an intuitive graphical interface for constructing and testing ETL procedures.

A number of end user tools and analytical databases come with crude ETL capability designed to get you started without the need for IT involvement or specialist tools. This may be appropriate for the *Extract* and *Load* part of ETL, or for moving well-organised data from the DW into a query tool or analytical database. However, ETL functionality tied to a specific end user tool does not increase availability of the data to the organisation as a whole. You may also find that complex data *Transformations* are difficult to achieve with bolt-on ETL tools and even more difficult to troubleshoot if they do not provide the expected results.

Good ETL tools automate or semi-automate the majority of common data manipulation tasks and provide significant productivity gains over bespoke programming solutions. The reality in the early stages of a BI strategy is that you will spend the majority of your development time doing ETL. For this reason, you want to be sure you perform the ETL work as efficiently as possible.

User interaction

In Chapter 1, we briefly considered a number of potential user groups for BI. I stated that each group would benefit from different BI tools and interactions styles. In the following sections, I discuss each of the user interaction tools in the generic BI solution architecture and provide guidance for their use.

Reports

Static and parameterised reports are not at the glamour end of the BI toolset. It is easy to overlook a specialist report-writing tool because it may be possible to produce reports using a spreadsheet or dashboard interface.

Report writer tool

I recommend that you include a specialist report writing tool in your solution architecture because they provide the best support for complex layout, consistent presentation, pagination, report scheduling, pixel perfect rendering and printing, various export formats, controlled parameters, and integration into other applications.

One common application of a report writer is to automate reports previously generated in spreadsheets. A good reporting tool should be able to replicate an existing report format precisely. This may be crucial if the report is for a supplier or a submission to a government authority. Specialist dashboard tools struggle with this kind of task. They have limited layout capability, do not support fine-tuned pagination, or cannot export to the required format.

Report proliferation

There is nothing more depressing to a BI specialist than a 100-page report reeling off the printer destined for someone's in-tray (trashcan). I cannot think of any justification for producing a 100-page report, let alone printing it.

Another woe of the reporting world is the situation where we produce dozens of routine reports– either manually or with a reporting tool – and deliver them by email to all and sundry without regard for their usage or relevance.

In both of these instances, the lack of focus undermines the value of the information. In the first case, it is clear that a 100-page report will not efficiently support any decision process because of the effort required to find relevant content, coupled with the risk of missing the pertinent information. In the second instance, we cannot accurately gauge whether the report is useful and who might benefit from more focused support.

BI in practice

The dangers of unfocused reporting

A company distributes a large stock inventory report to all the warehouse managers on a weekly basis. The report has a section for each warehouse containing all the products for that warehouse sorted in product order.

The warehouse manager goes to the section in the report that relates to the warehouse they manage and looks at the stock for each product. Each section has hundreds of lines for all the different products. The warehouse manager looks through the report to determine products that are low on stock.

Unfortunately, a data entry error has resulted in some products without an allocated warehouse. Because each warehouse manager only considers the section in the report relevant to their warehouse, the unallocated products go unnoticed until some are totally out of stock, resulting in an investigation.

It is clear that the report does not support the business process because it forces the recipients to analyse a large amount of irrelevant data to complete their task. The more noise in a report the less likely genuine issues will be noticed.

Ad hoc query

Ad hoc query tools are at once a blessing and a curse. The great selling points are that they take little configuration, give users ultimate flexibility, and provide a usable way of exploring the data. The user community often insist that an ad hoc query tool is the first and only required deliverable. Given the apparent ease of deployment, solution designers are happy to comply.

Complete reliance on ad hoc query tools is a sign that something is missing in the *business intelligence cocktail*. It can also result in a lot of unnecessary development work as the solution tries to cater for all eventualities. The advantages of ad hoc tools are immediately apparent but the disadvantages are more subtle and benefit from further discussion below.

Business goal

Ad hoc query tools do not directly support a business goal or decision. Where someone uses the tool in an unstructured way for regular decisions there is no easy way to measure the effectiveness of the decision process. Where someone uses the tool to produce a regular report or analysis, we should capture the procedure and deliver the content using automated reports or dashboards. This will guarantee the consistency of approach and remove repeated manual effort.

A legitimate use of ad hoc query tools is to respond to a new opportunity, line of enquiry, or prototype a new solution. All too often, the recipient of an ad hoc query then requests that the information is delivered on a regular basis, but we continue to produce the report using the same manual methods.

Performance

Ad hoc queries on small or simple data models generally have very good query performance. However, when you introduce algorithmic calculations or complex data relationships into the mix, query performance can suffer and server resources may be strained.

Ad hoc query analysis is very resource inefficient. Typically, the user will execute a large number of redundant queries in order to arrive at their final destination; this consumes time and server resources. Slow query response time frustrates the immediate user and potentially denies good service to other users sharing the same infrastructure.

Data model usability

Ad hoc query tools shift the complexity of implementation from the front-end tools into the data model. Users become frustrated that the data model is not easy to use, or where ease of use is not a problem, they find it is not powerful enough to answer all their requests.

It is very difficult to create a data model that captures all the complexities of a domain and is immediately intuitive to non-technical users. Manipulating the data or storage model to the advantage of one set of users can have an equally detrimental impact on another.

Even a simple data model will yield unintuitive results if the user does not understand the nuances of the underlying business rules. When we create a structured deliverable, like a report or dashboard, we can augment charts and tables with comments or description to clarify their meaning. Many analytical databases provide support for augmenting the data model with descriptive metadata but often this is insufficient to avoid ambiguity and misinterpretation completely.

Presentation of information

The value of information lies as much in its presentation as its content. If the instructions for a piece of self-assembly furniture have ever frustrated you, then you have had firsthand experience of this axiom.

Ad hoc query tools place the responsibility for layout and presentation firmly in the lap of the user. It can be time consuming to present data at different levels of granularity or subject areas side by side for comparison. The most interesting patterns in data seldom present themselves in simple summaries that are easy to produce using ad hoc tools.

Ad hoc query – final words

Despite the shortcomings of these tools, I would still advocate providing ad hoc query tools to anyone who feels they might benefit from them. The best way to prevent inefficient use of these tools is by promoting alternatives as part of the deliverables in each project. If the advantages are compelling then behaviour will change without the need to be prescriptive.

Spreadsheets

Just about every BI tool on the market will claim to support spreadsheet interaction. This is not surprising because many users judge the power of a BI tool by analogy to the functionality of their spreadsheet application. This is a very high bar because spreadsheet applications have become extremely powerful BI tools in their own right. Not surprisingly, some BI vendors have cut out the middleman by providing tight integration within the spreadsheet environment; the tool effectively extends the existing functionality of the spreadsheet application. Other BI applications simply export text files, which you can open and edit with a spreadsheet application in the normal way.

If the business community are spreadsheet gurus then nothing short of full spreadsheet functionality will satisfy them. In this case, I would advocate using an analytical database or BI tool with tight spreadsheet integration where the users can work directly with the BI tool and data within the spreadsheet environment. Using these tools, users can quickly automate routine reporting and analysis because they are already familiar with the spreadsheet tool and data. They can continue to use the spreadsheet to create the layout and presentation but the content will now update automatically when the underlying source acquires new data. There are a growing number of offerings in this space so it is worth researching the alternatives.

If spreadsheet integration is a priority then you should inspect candidate tools closely for this functionality. If the BI tool simply exports data to a spreadsheet format this is less than ideal as users will still have to perform manual data integration and routine formatting in the spreadsheet environment. We may just exchange one manual process for another.

Dashboards/Scorecards

Anyone who has seen a vendor presentation of BI tools will be familiar with executive dashboards. They have colourful gauges and traffic lights indicating the status of the business KPIs. The user can click on a KPI visualisation and drill down to a lower level of detailed data that explains the high-level trend. Whilst there is some debate amongst practitioners about the best way of visualising KPIs, most agree that dashboards and scorecards are a very effective delivery channel when carefully designed.

My personal experience is that dashboards work as well, if not better, for supporting operational processes as they do for executive level summaries. Operational dashboards have a narrower focus making it easier to source the data in the early stages of a BI program. Events tend to move quickly at an operational level and a dashboard can provide high visibility of changes and anomalies.

A real issue with executive level dashboards is finding the balance between providing a holistic view of the organisation whilst creating something that is responsive to events. If the metrics in the executive dashboard change infrequently or imperceptibly, executives will look at them once or twice and then move on.

Dashboard tools

Dashboard tools share some interesting characteristics with movies and computer games. Great graphics and special effects look amazing on the trailer and hold your interest for the first ten minutes of the film. But after the initial high, we want to engage with the storyline and the characters. If there is no substance underlying the flashy effects, we will quickly lose interest. Dashboard tools are the same. Many of them have amazing visualisations that instantly wow the audience. However, keep in mind that users are interested in something that will support their primary business goal. They will certainly be curious to see the latest gadget, but will not come back for more unless it helps them with their work.

It is important to separate the process of dashboard design – which is analytical and business oriented – from the implementation and delivery channel, which could as easily be a static document as a specialist BI tool. The impressive data manipulation features of dashboard tools will be most useful for analysts who can correctly interpret the impact of slicing and dicing the data. If senior managers and executives are your target audience, they may not appreciate or use these features.

Remember, the hardest part of implementing dashboards is deciding the content and integrating the data. Once we complete this preparation work, a good dashboard tool will provide a user-friendly interface for designing the layout and visualising the data. With this in mind, we should assess the strength of a dashboard tool by considering the:

- Usability of the design interface
- Flexibility of layout
- Support for a wide variety of chart types and visualisations
- Ability to realise a conceptual design

It is difficult to evaluate these criteria from a vendor demonstration alone, because most presentations focus almost exclusively on the end user interaction with the final dashboard design. The level of end-user interactivity of the dashboard tool may be important but we should also remember the primary purpose of the tool and the target audience. You may be judging the dashboard product with the criteria for an ad hoc analysis tool.

Some products integrate a dashboard tool with an analytical database engine – the data must be in the vendor's database to use their dashboard tool. In this instance, you should ensure that the database component is capable of supporting all the data and calculations you require in the dashboard.

Dashboard design

Dashboard design has two phases. Firstly, we must decide the information content. Secondly, we must decide how to present the information to the dashboard audience. Few (2006)[18] is the best starting point for looking at presentation and visualisation of dashboard data. The focus of this section is on the first step where we must decide which data, KPIs and summaries we want to include. Scorecard methodologies may help shape the information content in particular scenarios. However, my experience is that the myriad of possibilities can overwhelm users if we ask them to start with a blank sheet of paper.

To assist with the early stages of design I have developed a two stage structured approach to dashboard design[19]. The technique provides good coverage of the data and a framework within which users can develop their requirements. The approach does not assume a particular BI product. Most reporting and dashboard tools that I have used have the requisite functionality.

In stage 1, I identify important business entities and create simple summaries of events and measures that describe the interaction between them. This provides high visibility of the data and supports reconciliation and quality checks in preparation for stage 2. Stage 2 assumes the users have validated the simple data summaries in stage 1. I can now present complex derived measures with the confidence of a solid foundation. A common mistake of the dashboard process is to move straight to stage 2, before users have validated the raw measures and

---

[18] See *Recommended reading*
[19] This methodology is explained in detail in my forthcoming book, *Dashboard Design: A Structured Approach*

had a chance to interact with the dashboard tool. The following sections provide a quick summary of my approach.

Stage 1 – Part 1 Identify master data entities
Let us assume a simple manufacturing company. It has a single factory where they build the company's products. Wholesale customers order products through sales offices distributed throughout various regions. The customers are responsible for collecting the goods from the factory. From this description, we identify customer, product and office (which we report by region) as the master entities that drive the business.

Stage 1 – Part 2 Create simple dashboard and report
For each of the important master entities we design one dashboard and one list report. The list report has one row for each entity member. For example, the customer list would display one row for each customer. Each row in the list report is a link to the dashboard report for that member. Therefore, if you select *Customer A* on the list report you navigate to the dashboard report for *Customer A*. The table below provides the complete set of reports and dashboards we need to create for our example.

Table 14 - Dashboards and list reports to develop for the example company using the structured approach

Report name	Parameters	Links to
Customer list	Time period, set of customers	Customer dashboard
Customer dashboard	Time period, customer	Product dashboard/list, Region dashboard/list
Product list	Time period, set of products	Product dashboard
Product dashboard	Time period, product	Customer dashboard/list, Region dashboard/list
Region list	Time period, set of regions	Region dashboard
Region dashboard	Time period, region	Customer dashboard/list, Product dashboard/list

Figure 14 and Figure 15 show a possible layout for the stage 1 customer dashboard and list report.

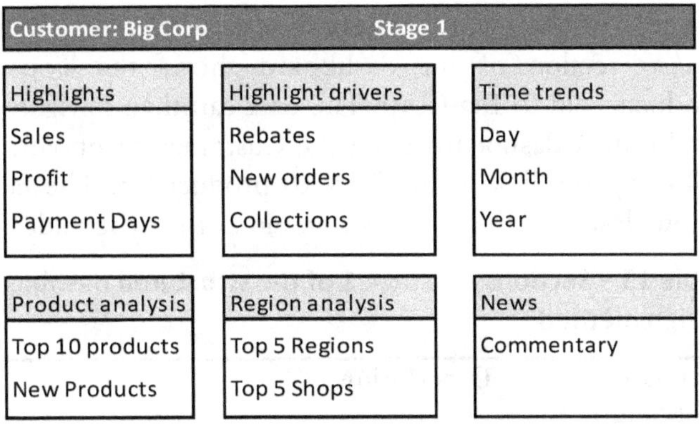

Figure 14 – Stage 1 entity dashboard

Customer List		
Name	Sales	Profit
General Inc	100	20
Acme Toys	70	10
Big Corp	300	60

Figure 15 – Stage 1 entity list

The list report can have any number of columns but we should select them on their ability to differentiate lines in the report. We use the list report to select an item to display in the dashboard. For example, a user analyses the list report, sees that Big Corp has the highest sales, and selects the Big Corp row to link to the customer dashboard for Big Corp.

The dashboard can have any number of sections and each section can contains graphs, individual figures, and tables. Each dashboard should have at least one section that shows the relationship between the entity in focus (customer in the example above) and the other master entities (product and region). For example, the *Product analysis* section of the dashboard shows the Top 10 products sold to Big Corp. The user can then navigate to the Product dashboard from the Customer dashboard by following the link in the Top 10 product list. The table below describes the sections I would normally include.

Table 15 – Sections for stage 1 of the structured dashboard design method

Standard dashboard section	Description
Highlights	The key measures of interest to the business or relevant to the entity in focus
Highlight drivers	Secondary measures that influence the key measures in the Highlights section
Time trends	Normally line graphs or bar charts showing the trend of some Highlight measures over time for the selected period
Product analysis	Shows the important relationships between the customer and the products e.g. the Top 10 products the customer buys
Region analysis	Shows the important relationships between the customer and the region e.g. a list of regions the customer buys from
News	Commentary or news relevant to the customer

In stage 1, we are not interested in sophisticated derived metrics. We just want to give users simple summaries so that they can browse and validate the data. Once the users can see the simple trends and summaries they are in a better position to define the more complex KPIs and derived measures that we introduce in stage 2.

Stage 2 – Part 1 Introducing more sophisticated metrics and KPIs
In stage 2 we can retain the same dashboard structure and mapping between entities and reports but rather than simple summaries we use more complex metrics and algorithms to move closer to the decision points that drive the business processes associated with the entity.

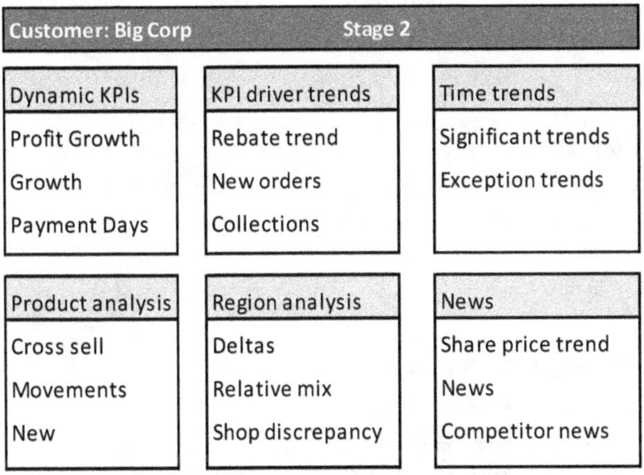

Customer: Big Corp	Stage 2	
Dynamic KPIs	**KPI driver trends**	**Time trends**
Profit Growth	Rebate trend	Significant trends
Growth	New orders	Exception trends
Payment Days	Collections	
Product analysis	**Region analysis**	**News**
Cross sell	Deltas	Share price trend
Movements	Relative mix	News
New	Shop discrepancy	Competitor news

Figure 16 – Stage 2 entity dashboard

Table 16 – Sections for stage 2 of the structured dashboard design method

Dashboard section	Description	Example
Dynamic KPIs	Targets that are dynamically linked to the market or performance of a related group of entities	Profit growth compared to average profit growth for all customers in the same region and industry type

Dashboard section	Description	Example
KPI driver trends	Movements in the underlying measures that will have recently influenced the KPIs	Rebates as a percentage of revenue up 5% on parallel period in previous year
Time trends	Trends that are significantly different to expected trends	Orders up 20% above average order growth for similar customers in same period
Product analysis	Complex relationships between customer and product	Customers with similar attributes to this customer bought more of these products (as a % of total spend) than the current customer
Region analysis	Complex relationships between customer and regions	Regions whose growth is lower than other regions and lower than average growth for similar customers in that region
News	Market data relevant to the customer or industry sector	Customer announces merger with another company. Possible opportunity for new sales due to growth through acquisition

We can also amend the list report to allow selection of entities based on metrics and KPIs. Ideally, the user should be able to sort the list report by each of the columns so they can quickly identify interesting rows in the list. We should also provide the choice of more focused list reports. An example might be a list of all customers who are significantly under their sales target.

Stage 2 – Part 2 customising for user requirements and business processes

The previous steps in the process should provide users with a good grounding in the possibilities inherent in dashboard design. They should now have enough familiarity with the tool and method to start creating their own dashboard designs.

We have aligned the dashboards to business entities, but we may create specialisations of these dashboards for each business process. For instance, we might create a customer dashboard for sales, and then another dashboard design for working capital. We could do the same for region. Marketing managers will be interested in the customer centric view. Office managers will want to know how their region is tracking.

Strengths of a dashboard approach

Having considered a structured method for dashboard design, we look now at some of the non-functional advantages of this approach. Dashboards are often a more focused alternative to ad hoc query tools so we make comparisons between the two styles where appropriate.

Data validation

Data preparation for DW and BI normally involves some degree of data transformation and the application of business rules. Domain experts will need to validate the data before it can reliably support decision making and more complex applications like data mining. Dashboards provide a user-friendly interface to the data. Reviewing aggregate values and graphs makes it easier to spot issues and outliers than generating random ad hoc queries. The structured approach used to create the dashboards also lends structure to the validation process, providing consistent views of the data and good coverage. We can design a validation plan using the dashboard reports with various parameters.

Usability
Ad hoc tools are powerful in the right hands but require the users to have a good knowledge of both the tool and the semantics of the data model. For example, multidimensional databases are particular vulnerable to misinterpretation. There are often large empty spaces in the cube and certain selections (slices) of dimensions can present unintuitive results. Good dashboard design allows us to assimilate the information quickly. We expose several perspectives that would be time consuming to construct manually.

Performance
Dashboard queries have a fixed structure with a number of parameters. This results in a predictable workload for the database. A predictable query workload is essential for database optimisation.
Ad hoc analysis may also follow standard paths of exploration but there is no constraint to say they must. Users generate a large number of intermediate queries getting to the view they are interested in. Inexperienced users may unintentionally launch complex queries that drain server resources and deny quick service to other users. Slow response time in the initial releases may turn your sponsors off the solution. In contrast, consistently good query response time in the early releases will give

users confidence in the solution; this is far easier to achieve through structured dashboards than managing ad hoc access.

Security

Ad hoc query tools often rely on the security model of the underlying database. Analytical databases can support a number of complex security scenarios but there are limitations. Complex scenarios may affect query performance and it may be difficult to validate that the security model behaves as required.

It is easier to align security in the reporting layer with business processes. BI solutions often utilise data from multiple business units and functions unrelated to the user. It is difficult to define this type of security at the data layer.

Business applications

One of the challenges of BI is getting people to use it. Analysts and power users aside, the majority of people are not interested in BI as a concept; they just want to get on with their jobs. There is no point having reports and dashboards tucked away at the end of an obscure URL, because users simply will not visit them.

Embedding BI into an existing application is one of the best ways to expose the functionality to users. Online retailers are the most visible example of this. When they suggest additional products that might be of interest based on our previous purchases, they do not ask the user to go to the analytics webpage. Instead, they seamlessly integrate the product recommendations – which may be the result of a market basket data mining model – into the existing process of buying an item or browsing a catalogue.

Data mining models within business applications are not restricted to retail product recommendations. Risk profiles for customer loan applications and fraud monitoring of credit card transactions are common examples of where BI is working in the background to support a business application.

Email

Email is probably the simplest example of delivering BI via other applications. Most people will check their email regularly and this provides the opportunity to get their attention with some timely information. Unfortunately, because it is simple, it is often overused. We are all quick to react to spam-mail. If the messages are not immediately actionable, there is a good chance users will redirect the mail to archive folders. We should reserve email for urgent and infrequent events.

Intranet

Most companies have a corporate intranet as the default homepage for web browsing. A tailored menu with alerts or links to useful BI applications embedded within the home page is a straightforward way to expose BI functionality. There will probably be a huge amount of information competing for space and attention on the homepage. If we only display the links or alerts when they are most relevant to the user – for instance after month end reporting – then they will have more impact.

Spreadsheets

We have noted on several occasions that spreadsheets drive many operational processes. If we are able to customise menus and toolbars in the spreadsheet applications, we can embed links to extended BI functionality within the spreadsheet environment.

Operational systems

Modern operational systems will generally provide a level of customisation. This may not be as straightforward as modifying an intranet page or sending an email but it has the distinct advantage of embedding the BI functionality directly into the heart of the business process. If you cannot modify the operational system, another option is to wrap the operational system interface inside a portal and present the BI application information within the same portal.

Business intelligence tool selection

When I think back on my experience I have seen little to suggest that the choice of one vendor's BI software over another was the key driver of a successful project. More important are the cooperation between stakeholders and developers, and the expertise of the team in the software at hand. Another vital step is matching the business problem with the correct component within the generic solution architecture. By example, budgeting and forecasting projects frequently use an analytical database because this technology makes it easy to spread revenue and costs dynamically, create complex time-based calculations, and support what-if scenarios.

When we are choosing between tools from different vendors we need to be sure that we are comparing like with like. For instance, we may love the interactivity and graphics of one vendor's dashboard tool and be disappointed by another vendor's report writing tool that lacks these features. This might seem like a blunt comparison but it is sometimes difficult to determine exactly what we are getting.

Vendors are keen to show their software as capable of every requirement but realistically most tools are very strong at a particular function and provide basic support for others.

Populating the business intelligence solution architecture

The technology strategy should aim to have one or more distinct tools available for each of the components in the generic BI solution architecture. The optimum number of distinct tools depends on the component and the table below provides some high level guidance for each one.

Table 17 – Software acquisition guidance for the components in the generic BI solution architecture

Tool/ component	Relative cost	Distinct tools per org.	Usage learning curve	Example application
ETL	Med-High	1	Med	Data integration and availability
DW RDBMS	High	1	Med	Historical data repository and data availability

Tool/ component	Relative cost	Dis-tinct tools per org.	Usage learning curve	Example application
Analytical database	Low-Med	1-2	Med	Budgeting, profitability, business modelling, trend analysis
Data mining	Low-High	1	High	Discovering trends and patterns in data
Report Writer	Low-Med	1	Med	High quality scheduled reports with complex fixed layout
Dashboard / Scorecards	Low-Medium	1-2	Low-Medium	High quality fixed layout with some interactive features
Interactive reporting and ad hoc analysis	Low	1-3+	Low	Business analysis
Spread sheet tool	Low	1	Low	Business process support and ad hoc analysis

Product evaluation

To make an informed decision about a product we must first understand what we are evaluating. Most BI vendor presentations will sound like they are selling an end-to-end BI platform. Dig deeper and you may find they are actually providing a front-end user tool and the consulting expertise necessary to extract your data and present it in the tool. There is nothing wrong with purchasing a product like this but at the end of the process, you will have an end user tool and some available data but you may not have an ETL, DW, or analytical database solution that you can use independently of the user tool for other projects.

Many BI products sold today are hybrids of one or more components in the generic architecture. One example is the analytical database that comes with some rudimentary ETL capability. This is fine and can add to the ease of deployment and maintenance for a particular solution. However, in the medium term, my experience is that a mature BI capability will require a distinct product for each of the components in the generic BI solution architecture.

We can build our capability with products from a single vendor or mix and match, but each component should operate as a standalone tool capable of integration with other product sets and data sources. In short, if you are not ticking all the boxes, do not blow the entire software budget!

Business intelligence vendors

BI vendors come in two flavours: enterprise platform vendors that cover the entire spectrum of BI components, and niche product vendors that specialise in a particular area[20].

Enterprise BI platform vendors

Enterprise BI vendors will provide a suite of integrated tools that cover most, if not all, of the components in the generic BI solution architecture. The potential advantages of the enterprise platform are:

- ✓ Software licence and support covers an array of products that would otherwise have to be negotiated separately
- ✓ Components should integrate together without additional custom development *
- ✓ BI specialists will have knowledge of all the components if they specialise in that vendor's products

The potential disadvantages are:

- Cost, if you are paying for a large number of products that you do not need or do not have the expertise to use
- Quality of components within the product set may vary significantly. An enterprise platform vendor will want to tick all the boxes of the generic BI solution architecture. However, they may not be market leaders in many of the distinct categories in which they compete
- It can create a perception that there is no requirement for further tools. This makes it more difficult to justify niche tools if the product set is perceived to be the complete solution or has taken the whole budget

---

[20] See http://www.bi-survey.com or http://www.gartner.com for more information on specific vendors and tools

* Do not take seamless integration of products for granted on any enterprise platform. There has been a lot of M&A activity in the BI industry during recent years and not all tools offered as part of an integrated platform will have grown up together.

Niche product vendors

There are many niche vendors in the BI market, particularly in the area of end user tools. The focus of the vendor will be on usability and look and feel because this is what sells BI products. These products can be an excellent investment, especially those that are inexpensive.

Specialist vendors can survive in the BI market – now dominated by large technology firms – because their products often provide functionality or a particular style of interaction more effectively than the equivalent offering in enterprise solutions. Some advantages of these tools are:

- ✓ Usability of the tools is often very high. Unlike enterprise vendors, niche players generally trade power and flexibility for simplicity. They aim to fulfil the target user group's common requirements without complicating the tool with integration or scalability features that enterprise tools must provide
- ✓ Cost of licence, training and deployment should be significantly cheaper than the equivalent tools as part of an enterprise platform
- ✓ Innovation often comes from small players in the market. Enterprise vendors will eventually provide functionality that is popular in the market

but there could be a lag of several years before
they catch up

On the surface, some of the niche vendor products
encapsulate the full functionality of the generic BI
solution architecture. They can have their own data
storage capability, data import tools, calculation and
presentation layer. However, there are inevitable
compromises and my experience is that no single product
can satisfy all the requirements of a mature BI capability.
Common weaknesses of these niche vendor tools are:

- ETL is limited, not user friendly, and with very
  basic functionality for troubleshooting errors
- Proprietary data model and data storage are only
  accessible through the user interface supplied by
  the vendor
- Data model does not impose constraints or allow
  for fine-grained updating. If the data is not clean
  before it is loaded, the database may not provide
  any feedback to suggest a problem. Loading data
  incrementally over time may be possible, but
  backdated corrections may be difficult to manage
  without performing a full reload. This may not be
  an option if the extraction process takes point-in-
  time snapshots of the source systems
- Documentation and online communities are
  limited and not very comprehensive. Detailed
  knowledge transfer can only occur through the
  vendor's consultants

Tool selection criteria

Technology consolidation

A common concern of technology managers in medium
to large organisations is the proliferation of BI and

reporting tools, resulting in a maintenance and license-cost nightmare. For these good reasons, they would like to consolidate their technology infrastructure by shedding some of the apparent redundancy.

The extent to which this represents a real problem or an achievable solution depends on where the tool sits in the BI solution architecture. Put simply, the closer we get to the end user, the more likely and acceptable it is to have a diverse range of technology. Previous experience and personal preference are important contributors to whether a user group will accept a given end user tool. We cannot expect these factors to be common across all user groups in the company.

On the other hand, ETL and RDBMS used for DW and historical data storage are prime candidates for consolidation because:

- Most specialist commercial RDBMS and ETL software is fully capable of satisfying the requirements for small to medium DW and data storage requirements. Some products do some things better than others but the choice of one technology over another is unlikely to make or break a project

- Management of ETL and RDBMS generally sits within the IT department so it should be easier to harmonise technology within a single department

Usability

Usability is most important when considering end user tools. ETL and database tools are predominately for technicians and power users who are more willing to sacrifice simplicity for power. Usability should be the number one priority for anyone designing an end user BI tool. When looking at a dashboard tool for instance, you need to consider both the usability of creating the dashboard, and the end user experience. We briefly consider some of the factors that influence usability in the following sections.

Interaction style

In common with other areas of technology, BI tools come in generations, with each new generation raising the bar on intuitive styles of interaction. If during a tool demonstration you are thinking it looks clunky, run for the hills!

Performance

The query response performance is difficult to judge without full data volumes and business rules. However, the smoothness and responsiveness of the application is possible to assess in a demonstration.

Online community and documentation

Some vendors are far better at providing current, thorough documentation than others. During one product evaluation, I opened the latest user manual to find it was referring to sample databases and operating systems that were at least 5 years out of date. The manual took me on a nostalgic – but ultimately frustrating – journey to a time long gone. Another vendor shortcut is to provide an online community. This is fine if it is open (does not require an array of passwords to enter), moderated, and supplemented by high quality vendor-produced technical articles. But without proper support, it seems to be the equivalent of telling the kids to go and play nicely amongst themselves!

Detailed technical articles and online help are not so crucial for small discrete end user products with high usability. If the product is for simple ad hoc *slice and dice* then quality documentation is not as important.

Cost

At the time of the dot-com bubble in the late 1990s, there were probably only a handful of vendors with enterprise reporting tools and BI capability. To a certain extent, this is still the case with database management systems and ETL, but the market for analytical databases, dashboards, and reporting tools now has dozens of good products. The competition has driven down prices so it is worth getting quotes from a number of vendors.

ETL *and database tools*

ETL and database management software can be expensive so the first thing a company should consider is whether they have existing licenses as part of their operational systems. The other obvious advantage to this is that you will have in-house expertise.

Even within the ETL and database sectors, there is a very significant variation to entry cost between vendors. Most tools are functionally similar in the core competencies. The main difference is that the high-end tools will provide better support for scalability, administration, auditing and automation of common tasks.

High-end enterprise tools are immediately appealing, especially if you have the budget, because they tick all the boxes. However, by using them in the early stages of a project you have immediately raised expectations of the BI program by requiring a far higher value add to balance the initial investment. This will necessarily mean you have to take on longer and riskier projects to justify the expense. These are dangerous waters for an immature BI program.

I would always recommend starting with a more commoditised toolset and taking on projects that are within the realms of their capability. Once you are confident with the process and outcome, and are testing the limits of these technologies – which may not be as soon as you think – then move to the high-end tools.

End user tools

There are large differences in licence costs between different user-facing databases and tools but less discrepancy in their functionality. The golden rule with these tools is not to spend the entire budget on a single product. However appealing a user-facing tool is, it will not suit everyone. Expect to deliver BI through a variety of tools and channels. With this in mind, you do not want your end user tools to be expensive and there is no reason why they should be.

Some vendors bundle user tools with more expensive database and ETL licences and so this is a good place to start. I have found that niche vendors often do a better job of end users tools than the enterprise vendors do, so it is worth keeping some budget in reserve even if you decide on an enterprise platform.

Product maturity

Tools that have matured over time are generally a safer bet than new releases. This is especially the case if a major vendor has developed the tool because of a perceived gap in their product range. They will want to get the product to market as quickly as possible and will plan to build the full functionality into later releases. A new product may look enticing but the limitations may be undiscovered.

The public knowledge base may also be limited with new products.

On the other hand, an established tool that has not had a new version in the last 2-3 years may be coming to the end of its development lifecycle. If no future releases are imminent, it may be worth looking at competitor products with a more modern architecture.

Experience

Once a user is familiar with a tool, they become very loyal to it, taking the product from one place to the next. This frustrates the efforts of a company trying to get uniformity but does lead to innovation. Expertise in a BI tool coupled with domain knowledge is the nirvana for productivity in BI so we should accommodate additional tools if new employees bring specific technical expertise to the company. Aim for a company standard DW and ETL, but analytical databases and end user tools should be in the realm of the business users.

Business intelligence infrastructure

When you first start to implement the technology strategy, it may be sufficient to host all your BI components on a single server. In my experience, a single powerful off-the-shelf server is preferable to several budget servers. I make this point because hardware virtualisation enables server administrators to deploy server instances with a lower specification than a modern laptop. These small servers are not appropriate for BI development.

BI tools are resource hungry – we measure their efficiency in person-hours not CPU cycles. The resource utilisation pattern of BI is different from operational systems. The server will either be 80%+ utilised or not at all. It is common to schedule ETL jobs overnight, regular report processing in the early morning, with ad hoc querying and analytics running during the day. With server utilisation staggered over the course of the day, it makes sense that each discrete process has access to all the available hardware resources.

Environments and deployment strategy

The traditional approach to software development is to have different environments for development, user acceptance testing, and production systems. This provides distinct areas to build, test, and integrate new development work with the existing solution. There are several reasons why you may wish to modify and relax this traditional approach for your BI strategy. We will consider these in the sub sections below.

Data volumes

BI tends to deal with large data volumes. It is one thing to have several environments when you are managing a collection of code modules and a small volume of test data. It is quite another to replicate a multi-terabyte database across three environments to give realistic indications of performance and scalability. The peculiarities of BI development and testing mean users often find it hard to give feedback unless you are showing them up-to-date production quality data. Poor performance (often query response time) is one of the major reasons why BI solutions are under-utilised. If you are developing and testing with a subset of data, it is much more difficult to predict production performance.

Agile development

Power users may be discussing a business problem with a colleague one minute, and designing the solution the next. This extremely agile form of development is possible because power users understand the business domain and the capabilities and limitations of the data and technology. This pattern should be encouraged because power users will be a key source of innovation in any business. They can informally design and test new solutions without the resource sapping demands of a formal project process. If the solution is useful then this is the time to apply more rigour to the design and ongoing maintenance.

In practice, this means that the BI infrastructure and tools should be available directly to the power user. It is a crushing disincentive to using the BI environment if the power user must go through a highly bureaucratic process of authorisation and approval every time they want to introduce a new capability. The most likely outcome of restricting access will be that the development once again goes underground using personal databases and spreadsheets, instead of utilising more efficient specialist tools. The worst outcome is that this type of development is completely stifled.

Requirements volatility

Recall our discussion of the path to structured and measurable decision support as shown in Figure 17 (below).

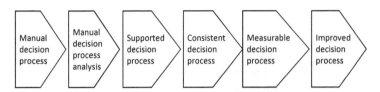

Figure 17 – The stepping stone path to decision support

Moving the BI solution from supporting the business process to driving it requires a continual cycle of development and feedback. Dashboards and reports will typically undergo a number of revisions before they arrive at the final design. Each revision and innovation opens the minds of users to further possibilities and brings the solution ever closer to supporting a point of action. Meanwhile by publishing the imperfect product in early iterations we still provide better support than if no solution existed at all. We should welcome and support this feedback loop. It is clear evidence that the users are actively engaged in the process. Sometimes change requests may seem superficial but as a rule, it is better to accept these and maintain an open dialogue, than introduce a formal change control process.

A lengthy deployment process can manage risk but at a high price. Users who accept some responsibility for the outputs in early iterations benefit tremendously from early exposure to the solution. My experience is overwhelmingly that users will be realistic and responsible in their use of the data and accepting of the limitations inherent in more advanced data manipulation and presentation.

Server resources and utilisation patterns

Given a fixed technology budget, it follows that as we increase the number of environments we reduce the budget allocated to each.

The pattern of utilisation for BI solutions is very different to operational systems. Operational systems support many concurrent users across a fixed number of constrained processes. Some BI processes may resemble this pattern but technologies like ETL, OLAP queries, and data mining model training will fully utilise a powerful server until the algorithm, query, or batch process completes. Because server utilisation is relatively infrequent but highly resource intensive, scheduling batch loads and complex data manipulation will make best use of server resources.

In the early iterations of BI projects, it is preferable to have one powerful server to support fast iterations of development, batch processing, and query response. The user community is likely to be quite small at this stage in the program. Shared access to resources is best managed through informal communication and scheduling of regular resource intensive processes outside working hours. As the user community and number of active projects grows, the increased sponsorship and utilisation of the BI platform will justify adding other environments.

Summary

In this chapter, we looked at the BI technology strategy. We covered:

- ✓ The components of the generic BI solution architecture
- ✓ Technology options for storing and processing data
- ✓ The different types of end user tools and advice on when to use them
- ✓ Criteria for BI tool selection
- ✓ BI server infrastructure and environment management

The key messages from the chapter are:

- ❖ Use the generic BI solution architecture to plan technology procurement. A mature BI strategy will have at least one distinct tool for each component
- ❖ Do not spend the entire budget with a single vendor in the early stages of the BI strategy. Whichever toolset you initially choose, gaps in functionality will emerge. It can be more cost effective to plug the gap with a specialist tool than try and bend existing tools to your requirements
- ❖ Aim for consistency for the data storage and ETL software but accept that you may need to support a range of end user tools to suit different interaction styles
- ❖ Remain open to niche vendor products even if you have already deployed a single-vendor enterprise BI platform

❖ Start with a single powerful off-the-shelf server rather than multiple low-end machines. Do not be too concerned about providing multiple environments for development, test, and production until you have completed several short projects

6.   Project management

Introduction to business intelligence project management

BI projects should be short and focused. BI tools exist to support a particular type of business problem or interaction. The challenge for a BI project is to combine the business problem, BI tools, and data without the normal overhead associated with bespoke application development. With this in mind, the focus of this chapter is to provide guidelines for individual project goals, duration, and participants, rather than a discussion of formal project management methodologies. Each BI project should contribute to all three pillars of the BI strategy by:

1. Improving a business process and raising awareness of the BI program
2. Increasing the availability of data in the organisation through ETL, DW, or simply raising visibility of the data
3. Demonstrating to users the potential of BI technology by supporting the business process with far less development effort than would have been required using regular software development

What do we cover in this chapter?

We start the chapter with a look at the recommended project duration and the breakdown of project time between process, data, and technology objectives. You may recall we looked at similar considerations when discussing BI capability in Chapter 2. Next, we look at the key participants in a BI project and relate this back to the *business intelligence cocktail* introduced in Chapter 1. Finally, I provide guidance on setting project goals so that we capture the full value of each discrete project. As with previous chapters, my intention is to discuss common issues, not provide a detailed implementation guide. If you execute short focused projects, you should be able to keep your formal project management overhead to a minimum.

Business intelligence project duration

In the first month of the BI program, we should run a number of discovery projects to introduce the three pillars of the BI strategy to the organisation and identify target business processes, data, and technology. Preferably, we should limit the scope of these discovery exercises to a single week's effort and duration. We could spend an infinite time on any one of these tasks but we want to gain just enough information to start a concrete project.

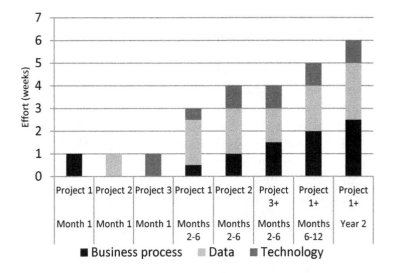

Figure 18 – Recommended project duration (weeks) and focus in the first year of the BI program

Figure 18 (above) shows an example of how you might structure BI projects in the first year of implementing your BI strategy. As discussed, we can use the first month to initiate each of the strategies. After the initial discovery projects, every full lifecycle BI project should provide some value to process, data, and technology strategies. At a minimum, each discrete BI project should:

- identify candidate business processes and whet the appetite of the business community for further process discovery
- improve availability of data by discovering, working with, and publishing data sources either as a virtual data dictionary or using physical data integration

- test the capabilities of the BI technology infrastructure and improve understanding of its use

Based on my experience I have shown a rough indication of the proportion of time that each of the strategies should consume within a project. The chart shows that data analysis and ETL – data strategy – typically consume much of the effort in the first few projects. However, as the data strategy matures we can tackle increasingly complex business problems and therefore the business process analysis takes an increased share of project time.

Business intelligence project focus

It may be tempting to devote entire projects to integrating and publishing data. This common mistake often stems from not managing business expectations in the initial stages. The business community may give the feedback that they are not interested in looking at the data until sources x, y and z, are fully integrated. This is an early sign of a BI project in troubled waters. The focus is not on the business goal but the data, and the user community are not showing active engagement in all stages of the project.

The sooner we can publish data to the users; the sooner we can introduce BI tools and receive feedback about the data quality. Each of the early projects should devote at least 20% (~1 week) of the time to deployment of ad hoc tools, dashboards and focused delivery of information.

If the user community want to engage, they will help overcome the inevitable data integrity and availability challenges. If they do not, then better to raise the red flag on the project at this early stage and move to another business function until conditions change.

Business intelligence project team

In Chapter 1, we described the ingredients of the *business intelligence cocktail*. Two key participants emerged; the subject matter expert, and the BI specialist. In the first few iterations of your BI strategy, you will definitely benefit from engaging BI specialists that understand the BI lifecycle and have experience in the selected toolset. They should work with the stakeholders, power users, and technology department to build an in-house capability. With each BI project, the organisation should take increasing ownership of the activities for eliciting requirements, development, and support.

BI projects should be short, especially in the first year, so project management should be lightweight. The most important project management steps are to determine the feasibility of the project and retrospectively analyse the outcome and lessons learned. A professional project manager may assume responsibility for the BI program, but if they are not available then the project sponsor, subject matter expert, or BI specialist can complete the management tasks for each individual project.

Team interaction

In Chapter 1, I stated my preference for direct interaction between the subject matter expert and the BI specialist. I also recommended that the subject matter expert is the person responsible for the business process or decision. In reality, many large organisations have a structure similar to the one below.

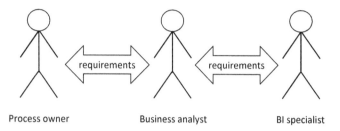

Process owner   Business analyst   BI specialist

Figure 19 – Standard communication model in large corporations

In this model, the process owner and the BI specialist have no direct contact. The process owner communicates with a business analyst and the business analyst communicates with the BI specialist. The business analyst is normally an expert in software lifecycle and design methodologies and understands the business processes. For this reason, the structure above works well for traditional software development where requirements pass through stages of conceptual design, technical design, and finally implementation.

BI projects have a different emphasis to traditional software projects because we are looking for opportunities to apply new technology to existing problems. In short, requirements take shape with direct reference to the capabilities of the tools. If we assume that the process owner and the business analyst are not experts in the BI technology, then we must also accept that they cannot generate BI requirements as effectively as they could if guided by the BI specialist.

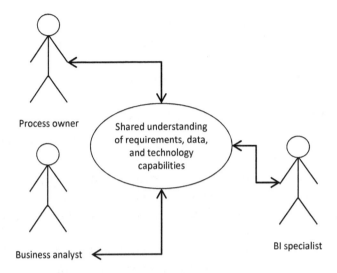

Figure 20 – Recommended communication model for BI projects

In my experience, a face-to-face discussion with the business process owner is the quickest way to determine where BI can add value to their process. If a business analyst is available then this discussion will be even more effective because of their ability to unravel business jargon, clarify ambiguity and provide context for the technology.

As the BI technology strategy matures, the business analyst will probably become expert in one or more BI tools. When this occurs then the business analyst can assume the role of the BI specialist, developing the BI solutions themselves in coordination with the subject matter expert. This is the ideal scenario for a BI strategy. The further we can extend the knowledge of the tools into the business, the more likely we will identify opportunities for innovation and process improvement.

When a new challenge arises that the business analyst cannot confidently resolve with the familiar toolset, this is a good time to re-engage a BI professional to evaluate whether other BI tools would provide a better fit.

Business intelligence project goals

We opened the chapter by stating that each BI project should contribute to all three pillars of the BI strategy. If we judge the success of a project within very narrow parameters, we increase the chance of a negative outcome. Conversely, if we aim to achieve a broad range of objectives that provide value for the process, data, and technology strategy it is very likely that the project will meet at least some of these goals within the project budget and timelines. This might seem like semantics, but in the early stages of implementing the BI strategy, perception is important to gaining sponsorship for future projects. No one benefits if sponsors cancel the entire program just weeks before we expect to deliver measurable business value, due to a negative perception of current progress.

It is a shame to hear of DW or BI projects deemed failures because they did not meet all the expectations of the business. When you look at the project in more detail, you find a lot of good DW and ETL work ready for use in future projects. The obvious, but nonetheless difficult objective is to manage expectations for the project from the beginning. The business will be primarily concerned with the process improvement objectives, but it is worth emphasising the project's contribution towards the data and technology pillars because this work will lay the foundations for tackling more complex business problems in future projects.

A straightforward way of setting project goals is to align each component in the BI solution architecture with an objective of the three pillars of the BI strategy. The following table provides some examples of this approach.

Table 18 – Setting objectives for a BI project

BI component/ activity	Project objective	% Project Estimate
Business process analysis	Process strategy – identify target business processes	20%
Source system analysis	Data strategy – increase visibility of data	10%
Data warehouse design	Data strategy – improve data structure of source data Technology strategy – build experience of DW software	10%
ETL	Process strategy – define business rules and automation Data strategy – increase data integrity Technology strategy – build experience of ETL software	20%-30%
Analytical database design	Process strategy – define business rules Data strategy – improve query performance and data structure Technology strategy – build experience in software and query language	10%-20%

BI component/ activity	Project objective	% Project Estimate
User tools	Process strategy – demonstrate report automation/business process support. Raise awareness of the program to attract new candidate business processes Technology strategy – raise awareness of capabilities	10%-20%

The focus of a project may be too narrow if it only includes a couple of activities in the table. We can normally add extra elements to the project with little additional effort. For instance, a project to create a daily extract from a source system may fail to deliver business value if there are unanticipated issues with the data. However, if we use the project to train new users in the ETL technology and create some exception reports with a new tool, then we have increased our capability to execute subsequent projects.

Data volumes and project goals

Response time is a key factor in user acceptance of a BI application. We have all cancelled a webpage request because we had to wait more than a few seconds for it to load. BI tools will suffer the same fate if they respond slowly to users requests. The need for speed guides the volume of data we should target. BI applications often use a large volume of historical data to provide trends and historical analysis. However, in early iterations of the BI program we should not be too ambitious.

On the one hand, we need to develop the BI application with the anticipated data volume to gauge the performance of the user tools. On the other, very large volumes of data add time and complexity to almost every aspect of the BI development process. We want to spend early BI projects adding business value and improving our process and capability with the tools, not wrestling with performance problems.

It can be difficult to judge what constitutes a challenging volume of data in advance of the project. It will depend on the tools, server infrastructure, and processing requirements. However, if more than 5% of the project time is spent performance tuning then this is an early warning sign to reassess the project objectives or design. In my experience, it is sometimes preferable to negotiate a compromise on data volumes part way through the project, rather than let performance tuning overtake the original objectives of supporting the business process.

Always remember that BI solution development should be fast and effective. When we apply BI technology to the right problem this is always the case. If it is not, we should redirect our effort to quicker wins and leave intractable problems until later in the program. At this later date, we will have increased our capability in the toolset, and may have redefined our approach to supporting the business objective based on project experience.

Summary

In this chapter, we have taken a brief look at project management in the early stages of a BI program. We discussed the:

- ✓ High level goals of each BI project and how they relate to the three pillars of the BI strategy
- ✓ Duration of BI projects and the indicative effort towards business process, data, and technologies strategy goals
- ✓ Interaction between the key team members of a BI project
- ✓ Approach for setting detailed project goals to reduce the risk of a failed project

The key messages from the chapter are:

- ❖ Every BI project should work towards the goals of all three pillars of the BI strategy
- ❖ Accept that data acquisition will consume the majority of time on early BI projects but avoid the temptation to focus solely on the data strategy. Expose the data to the users at the earliest opportunity
- ❖ Encourage direct communication between the BI specialist and business process owner. BI is about identifying opportunities for using technology and available data to meet existing requirements in a novel way
- ❖ Set goals for all the stages of the BI project and promote successful outcomes at this level as well as for the overall project
- ❖ Early BI projects are particularly risky because the data and technology strategies are still

immature. Unforseen data or technology issues may undermine our ability to support the original business goals but the project can still add value to the BI program. Ensure that stakeholders see the full value of every project iteration

❖ Large volumes of data add complexity to every stage of a BI project. Avoid scalability challenges in early iterations and focus on delivering business value within the limitations of a reduced data set

Final thoughts

BI technology will play an increasing role in our day-to-day business activities. We should welcome this trend because the technology does provide a solution for the business process problems that we are experiencing today. Every time we struggle with a complex business problem, unintuitive system, or lack of information and think, "There has to be better way", we take the first step towards a BI solution. There *is* a better way and all it takes are a few ingredients mixed together to create a solution to our problem and open our minds to the many other opportunities for decision support and process improvement.

Home office software revolutionised administration within the workplace. Email and the internet changed and extended effective communication. The latest operational systems capture ever-increasing data volumes. The combined impact of these advances is to shift the core competencies of the workforce from operational and clerical, to that of information management. However, these new responsibilities require a new set of tools. DW methodology provides a solution to information management but the challenges do not stop there. The information must be accessible to the people who understand and drive the business. BI technology is the new tool bag for the information worker and should be available to us all.

To those who think that BI technology is just for the cash rich blue chip companies, I say, research the BI technology market and see the affordable products and solutions. To those who think BI tools are a nice to have for the analysts and power users, I say, take time to investigate the processes of managers and operational professionals to see the efficiencies that could be realised. To those that think it is too hard and too risky, I say, start with small projects that build confidence and competence in the new approach.

A BI strategy is a natural consolidation of activities that take place in every productive business. We all strive to improve our processes, create accurate information, and use the technology to its best advantage. BI methods and the new generation of BI technology is the best route to achieving these objectives in the information workplace of today.

Glossary

Term	Description
3NF	See *third normal form*
BI	See *business intelligence*
Business intelligence	Business intelligence (BI) is the use of specialist technology for decision support and business process improvement
CRM	See *Customer relationship management*
Customer relationship management	A customer relationship management system (CRM) holds details of the organisation's customers and supports sales and marketing business processes
Dashboard	In the BI world, a dashboard is a way to present information using mainly graphical representations like charts, dials, and indicators. The dashboard analogy comes from a car dashboard where the driver has a clear view of all the important information they need for driving a car

Term	Description
Data availability	For BI, data availability encapsulates all those factors that influence the cost, time, or feasibility of obtaining data for a BI solution. Issues that affect data availability include visibility, data quality, security, and update timing
Data mart	A data mart is a dimensional modelling representation of a business process or event. It includes at least one fact table that holds transactions describing each instance of the event and a number of dimension tables that describe the participants to the event
Data warehouse	A data warehouse (DW) is a database that stores data from other sources for the purpose of analysis. By virtue of integrating data from various systems and recording changes in data over time, the DW will contain information that was never available or subsequently lost in the source systems and therefore the DW becomes far more than the sum of its parts
Data warehouse appliance	A product to support DW that includes the software and hardware as an integrated package

Term	Description
Dimension	In dimensional modelling, each dimension represents one or more entities that engage in events modelled by the facts. Typical dimensions are customer, supplier, employee, and product. Dimensions can also model general concepts like date/time and currency
Dimensional modelling	Dimensional modelling is the process of modelling data as facts (transactions/events) and dimensions (context for the facts). In a RDBMS, a dimensional model is called a star or snowflake schema because the graphical representation of the data model has a central fact table with various dimension tables branching out from it in the pattern of a star. The design resembles a snowflake if normalisation has been applied to the dimension tables.
DW	See *data warehouse*

Term	Description
Enterprise resource planning	Enterprise resource planning (ERP) software aims to integrate all of a company's core business processes into a single system. An ERP system removes the need to have separate systems for each business function. For example rather than having different systems for general ledger, human resources management, operations, and customer relationship management, an ERP system would provide all this capability in a single integrated package. Informally, the term ERP is often used to describe the company's main operational system, even if it does not incorporate all the business functions
ERP	See *enterprise resource planning*
ETL	See *extract, transform, load*

Term	Description
Extract, transform, load	Extract, transform, load (ETL) is a three stage process used in DW and BI development. The first stage extracts data from a data source, for example, an operational system or spreadsheet. The second stage transforms the data. This can include applying business rules, improving data quality, and integrating with other data sources. The final stage loads the transformed data to the destination; this might be a DW or BI tool
Fact	In dimensional modelling, a fact represents an event or transaction that occurs at a point in time. For instance, sales transactions translate to sales facts. Each sale is an event. Each fact record will hold values specific to the event like the cost and quantity of the item; these values are measures or fact attributes. A fact table is used to represent a fact in a RDBMS

Term	Description
General ledger	A General Ledger (GL) system supports the accounting and finance functions of a business that uses double-entry book keeping. The General Ledger system will contain a history of financial transactions, the chart of accounts, and current balances of each account
Human resources management	A Human Resources Management System (HRMS) supports typical employee lifecycle activities like hiring, performance management, training, and payroll
Key performance indicator	A key performance indicator (KPI) encapsulates one or more metrics and targets and defines the relationships between them. A KPI to measure sales growth is a simple example. The KPI will define the metric (sales growth over previous year) and the target (say 5%) and then report the variance between the target and actual results. The current value of the KPI can be represented a collection of discrete values (behind target, on target, above target) or as a continuous range

Term	Description
KPI	See *key performance indicator*
Master reference data	See *reference data*
MDX	MDX (multidimensional expressions) is a query language used to interrogate multidimensional databases. The MDX language exploits the rich metadata about hierarchies and relationships in the multidimensional data model to support analytical queries
OLAP	An OLAP (online analytical processing) product stores data for the purpose of querying and analysis. Typically, a single query will summarise thousands of transactions to provide trends and insights about the business. This differentiates an OLAP system from an OLTP system (online transaction processing) which is optimised for inserting, updating, and deleting individual records as part of an operational process

Term	Description
Primary data source	A primary data source, for the purpose of BI, is the source where the data is first collected and maintained. This may be different to what the organisation considers the master source of data due to update timings. For instance, a spreadsheet may contain information about sales agreements before they are updated in the operational system. BI solutions are interested in these primary sources because they are often available before the data is available in an operational system or DW
RDBMS	See *Relational database management system*

Term	Description
Reference data	Reference data is a term to describe any data that helps run the business but is not transactional. In a hospital, information about patients, drugs, hospital wards, and postcodes, would be classified as reference data. Master reference data is a term used to differentiate a particular class of reference data. It usually refers to data that is specific to the organisation. In a hospital, information about wards and doctors would class as master reference data, whereas a list of addresses in the hospital catchment area, would be classified as reference data
Relational database management systems	Relational database management systems (RDBMS) are software used to store and manage data using a relational model. Most operational systems use a RDBMS to store and retrieve the persistent data required by the organisation

Term	Description
Scorecard	A scorecard is similar to a dashboard in that it normally provides a succinct graphical view of the status of a business process, function, or the organisation as a whole. However, unlike dashboards there is an assumption that we are measuring (scoring) the subject area by comparison to predefined targets
Slice and dice	Slice and dice describes the user interaction style when viewing data in an OLAP cube. Users slice and dice the data to create a subset of the information in the cube. Typically, users slice and dice as part of ad hoc analysis. It allows them to generate different perspectives quickly to answer a question or find interesting trends
SQL	SQL (structured query language) is the language used to query and manipulate data in a RDBMS

Term	Description
Subject matter expert	For BI, the subject matter expert is the person who understands the business process and how it contributes to the goals of the organisation. They can be the one responsible for the outcome or operation of the business process, or an analyst who does not directly influence the process, but is responsible for monitoring the impact and effectiveness of the process
Third normal form	A relational database is in the third normal form (3NF) if all the non-key attributes for a given table depend upon the key attribute(s) in the table, and no other attributes. The method reduces duplication in the data model thus avoiding inconsistency

Term	Description
Transaction data	Transaction data concerns the events and activities of the organisation. Transaction data is not limited to financial transactions. In a hospital, transaction data would include information about admissions, surgical operations, and medicines prescribed to patients. All these events are point in time occurrences that involve interaction between the entities that describe the domain

Recommended reading

Few, S. (2006) Information Dashboard Design: The Effective Visual Communication of Data; O'Reilly Media Inc.

Imhoff, C. et al. (2003) Mastering Data Warehouse Design: Relational and Dimensional Techniques; Wiley Publishing Inc.

Inmon, W. H. (2005) Building the Data Warehouse, 4th ed.; John Wiley & Sons: Oct 2005

Kimball, R. and Ross, M. (2002) The Data Warehouse Toolkit: The Complete Guide to Dimensional Modeling 2nd Edition, John Wiley & Sons: New York 2002

Malinowski, E. & Zimányi, E. (2006) A Conceptual Solution for Representing Time in Data Warehouse Dimensions, The Third Asia-Pacific Conference on Conceptual Modelling (APCCM 2006)

Spofford, S. et al. (2006) MDX Solutions: With Microsoft SQL Server Analysis Services 2005 and Hyperion Essbase; John Wiley & Sons; 2nd Edition Mar 2006

Index

3NF, 87, 91, 108, 139
accounts clerk, 40
accounts receivable
   process, 31
ad hoc query, **149**–52,
   164
   ad hoc tools, 164
   security, 165
agile, 52, **180**
analytical databases, 126,
   140, 143, 169
   business rules, 125
   dimensional model,
      109
BI capability, 14, 29, 176
   curve, 49
BI consultant, 20
BI methods, 39
BI requirements
   decision point analysis,
      65
   defensive barriers to
      change, 65
   intractable problem, 63
   migration project, 78
   organisation chart, 61
   prioritising, 76
   stakeholder
      engagement, 76

volatility, 180
BI solution architecture,
   27, 47, **134**–37, 193
   business rules, 124
   tool consolidation, 174
BI specialist, **20**, 21, 189,
   190, 191
BI strategy, 14, **43**
   align to business
      strategy, 60
   IT department, 54
   managing
      environments, 179
   three pillars, 14, **43**
   use of spreadsheets,
      117
BI tools
   product maturity, 177
   selection, 132, **167**
   technology
      consolidation, **31**
   usability, 174
BI users, **34**
   analysts, 29, 37, 165
   customers, 37
   front line, 36
   intra company users,
      35

managers, 32, 36, 37, 120

senior managers, 36, 63, 77

suppliers, 37

budget, 12, 23, 56, 176, 182, 192

Building the Data Warehouse, 103

business analyst, 190

business applications, 36, 165–67

business goal, **18**, 20, 21

business intelligence cocktail, **17**, 76, 79

business rules, 39, **120**–27

data warehouse, 125

placement in the architecture, 124

call centre, 67

cash flow, 31

CRM, 25, 111

CSV, 91, 100

culture, 59, 98

culture of trust, 90, 99

dashboards, 22, 30, 36, 39, **153**–65, 169

dashboard design, 154, 156

data validation, 163

executive dashboards, 22, 28

performance, 164

usability, 164

data acquisition, 66, 120

data architecture, **137**–**47**

data availability, 19, 44, 77, 92, 116

data source structure, 90, 99

data warehousing, 105

non-existing data, 91, 100

security, 90

update timing, 93, 101

data integration, 29, 30, 114

data integrity, 87–89, 96–97

data mining, 36, **143**, 147, 166, 169, 182

analysing the results, 144

data ownership, **116**

data quality, 87–89, 96–97

data accuracy, 89

data security, 90, 97–99

data storage architecture, **137**

data strategy, 66, 71, **83**

data visibility, 93–96

spreadsheets, 118

data volumes, 179

impact on project, 194

data warehouse, 11, 100,
  102, **105**–13, 118, 168,
  192
  benefits, **106**
  modelling, **108**–11
  modelling time, 110
  one version of the
    truth, 122
data warehouse
  appliance, 138
decision support, 32, 33
deployment process, 181
deployment strategy, **179**
dimensional modelling,
  109
ease of doing of
  business, 37
email, 166
empowerment of users,
  51
environments, 53, 133,
  179
ERP. *See* operational
  systems
ETL, 77, 99, 113–15,
  125, 133, 146, 173,
  174, 185, 188
  tools, 176
Financial Controller, 23
General Ledger, 24
hardware, 13
Human Resources, 24
industry survey data, 92

infrastructure, 44, **178**
Inmon, 103
intranet, 166
IT department, 13, **52**
KPI, 21, 23, 27, 30, 67–
  76, 156
  defining KPIs, **67**
  defining metrics, 71
  dynamic KPI, 73–76
  identify data, 70
  KPI volatility, 28
  quantify the objective,
    69
  visualising KPIs, 72
manual decisions process, 33
marketing, 30, 92, 120
marketing analyst, 92
marketing director, 62
MDX, 91, 141
measuring business
  intelligence, 29
metric, 67–76
migration project, 78–79
migration projects, 78
OLAP. *See* analytical
  databases
one version of the truth, 13,
  121
online retailers, 11, 165
operational processes, 39
operational systems, 39,
  53, 100, 167, 176, 182
  BI support, 41

operations director, 62
organisation chart, 63
payroll system, 122
personal databases, 29,
    53
power users, 20, 29, 133,
    165, 180, 189
proactive BI, 22, 23, 35,
    38, 40
process analysis, 33
process automation, 31
process improvement,
    59
process improvement
    strategy, **59**
process owner, 18
product evaluation, **170**
project, 55, 66, 182
    duration, 77, **186**
    flexible deployment,
        52
    goals, 192
    maintain sponsorship,
        29
    management, 185–95
    moral, 56
    team, **189**
    team interaction, 189
qualitative value, **32**
quantitative value, **29**
Ralph Kimball, 103
RDBMS, 90, 91, 100,
    139, 168, 174

software, 176
    use as a data
        warehouse, 139
reactive BI, 21
real time information, 93
relational databases. *See*
    RDBMS
Report writer, **147**, 169
reports, 22, 29, 36, 126,
    147–49, 165
    as requirements
        specification, 78
    business rules, 125
    lifespan, 125
    report automation, **29**,
        30
    report proliferation,
        148
risk, 14, 56, 76, 98, 99,
    176, 181
sales representative, 18
scorecard. *See*
    dashboards
security, 90, 97–99, 165
server utilisation, 182
slave to the strategy, 55
social networking, 11, 99
spreadsheets, 13, 29, 53,
    152–53, 166
    ad hoc queries, 36
    as data source, 91
    managing, 117–20

pros and cons of use, 117
prototyping, 37
spreadsheet explosion, 117
SQL, 91
structured decision, 32
subject matter expert, 63, 189, 191
scope ETL work, 114
technology consolidation, **173**
technology strategy, **131**
The Data Warehouse Toolkit, 103

unstructured data, 99
user acceptance testing, 179
user interaction, 147–67
utilisation patterns, 182
vendors, 52, 168, 171, 177
Enterprise BI platform, 171
M&A, 172
niche product vendors, 172
web services, 13
XML, 91, 100

About the author

Colin McGowan is a business intelligence consultant with 10 years' experience designing and implementing decision support and process improvement solutions for organisations across a wide range of industries in London (UK) and Sydney (Australia). He has a Law Degree (LLB Hons), a Post Graduate Diploma in Software Development, and a Master's Degree in Computing. For his Master's Degree, he spent two years actively researching data warehouse modelling methodologies. Colin is the founder of CMBI (*colin mcgowan – business intelligence*), a business intelligence consultancy service based in Sydney, Australia, where he currently lives with his wife and family. If you have any feedback about the book, you can contact Colin at colin@cmbi.com.au or visit his website at www.cmbi.com.au.